Crescents

Theressa Silver

With an introduction by
Stephen B. Gerken

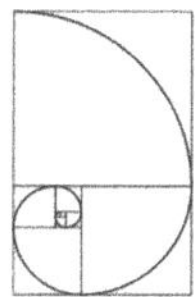

Theressa J. Silver Press
Oregon

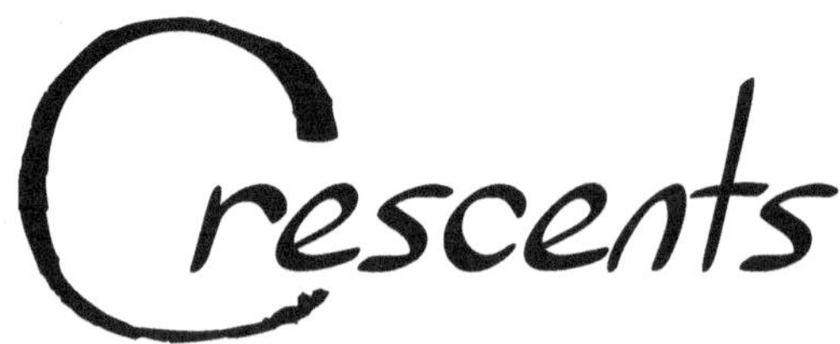

ISBN-13: 978-1-7335704-2-8

First Edition
Published by Theressa J. Silver Press

Copy Editor: Stephen B. Gerken
Model: Robin Gill
Sample Knitter: Kate Lindstrom
Test Knitters: Krashenne Asplodd, Su Fennern, Heather Hagen, Barbara Moncer, and Eva Schweber

Every effort has been made to ensure that all the information in this book is accurate at the time of publication. However, Theressa J. Silver Press neither endorses nor guarantees the content of external links referenced in this book.

If you have questions or comments about this book, or need information about licensing, custom editions, special sales, or academic/corporate purchases, please contact Theressa J. Silver Press: tsilver@spiretech.com

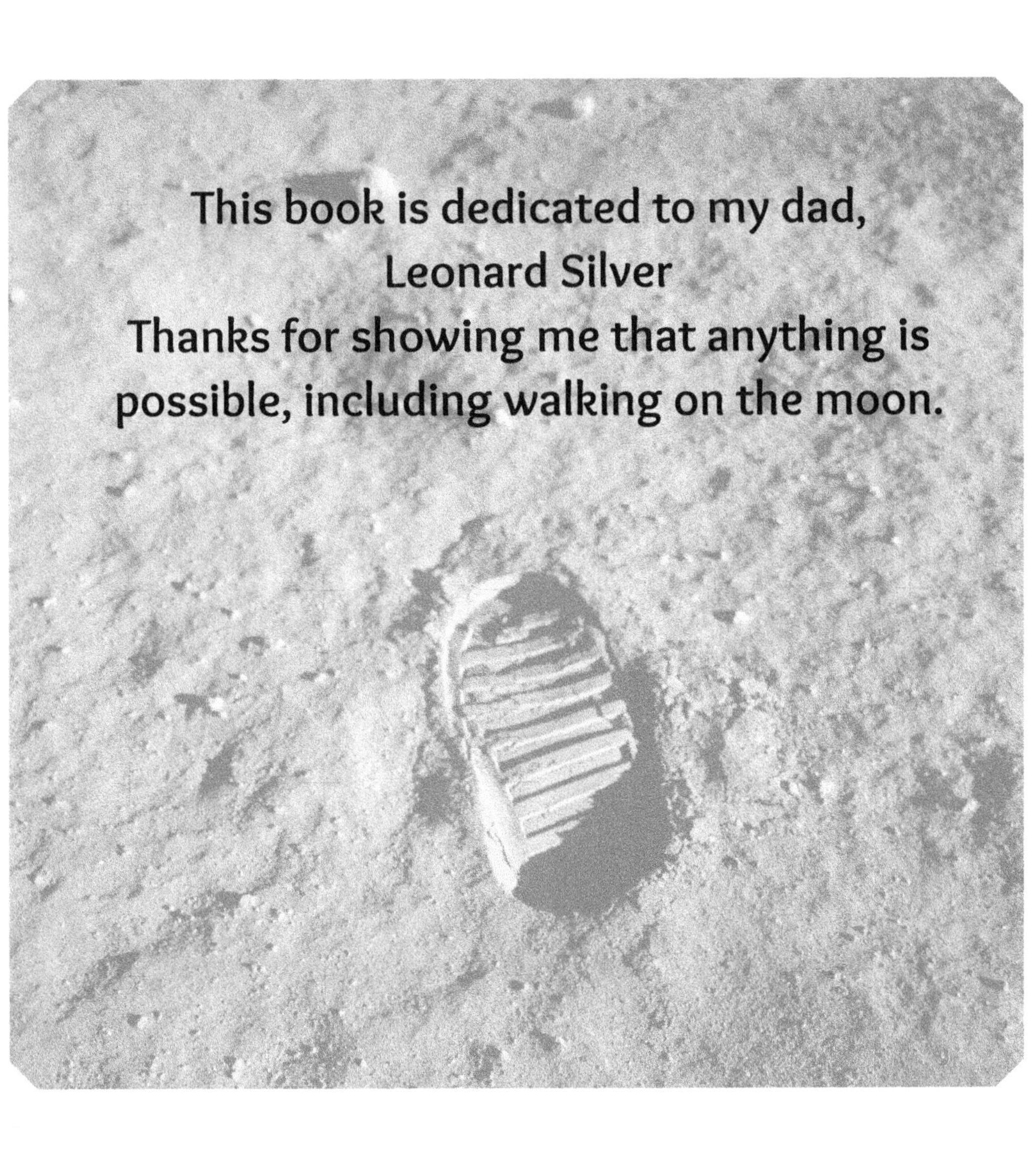

This book is dedicated to my dad,
Leonard Silver
Thanks for showing me that anything is
possible, including walking on the moon.

Contents

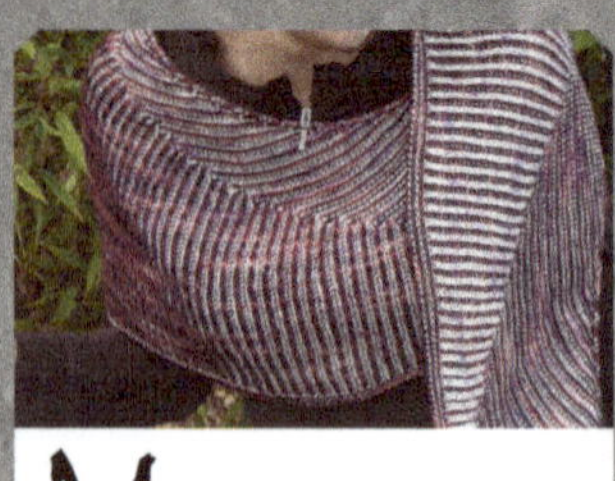

Moonrise   11

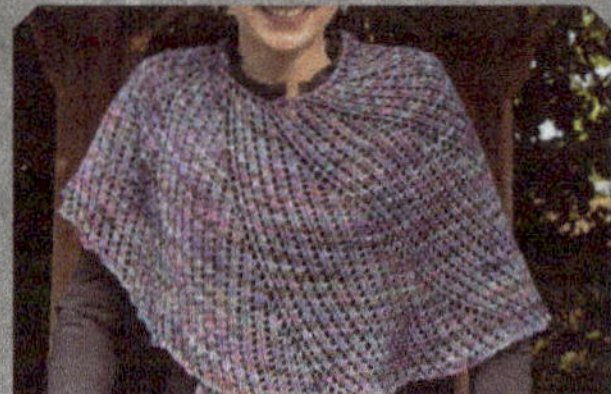

Moonbeams   17

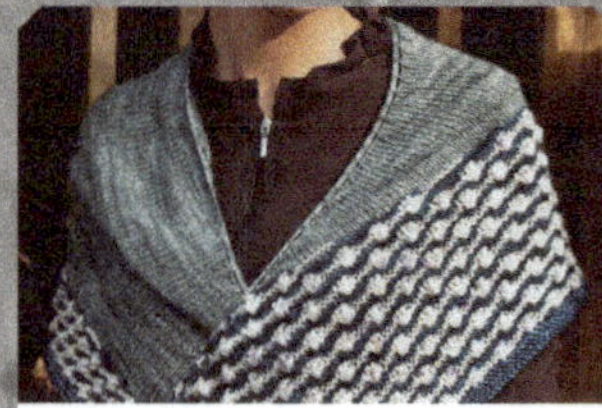

Earthrise   23

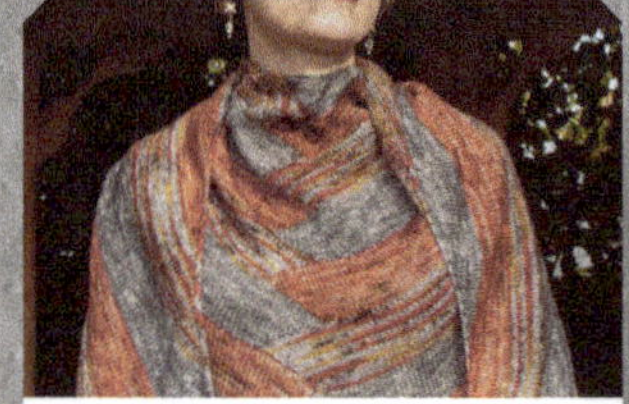

Eclipse   27

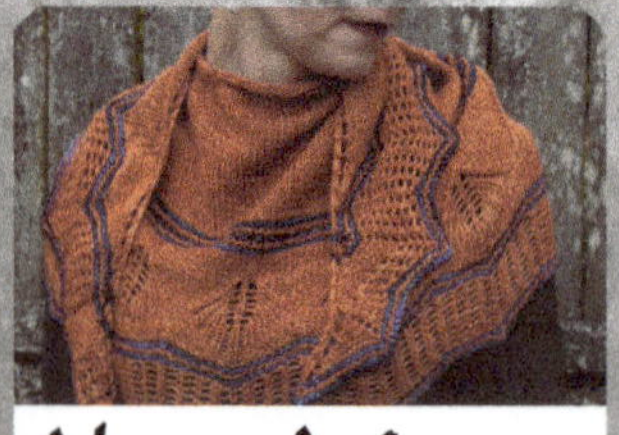

Harvest Moon   33

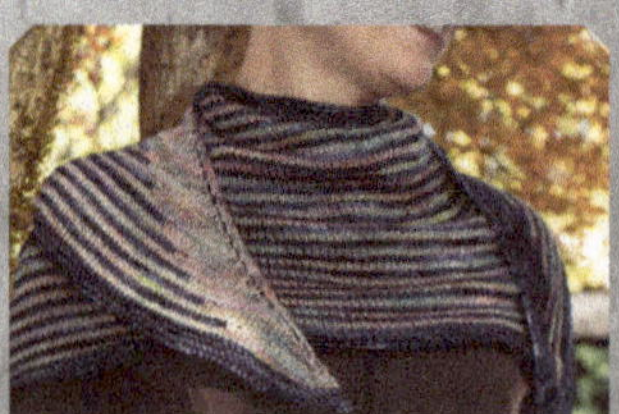

Moonbow   41

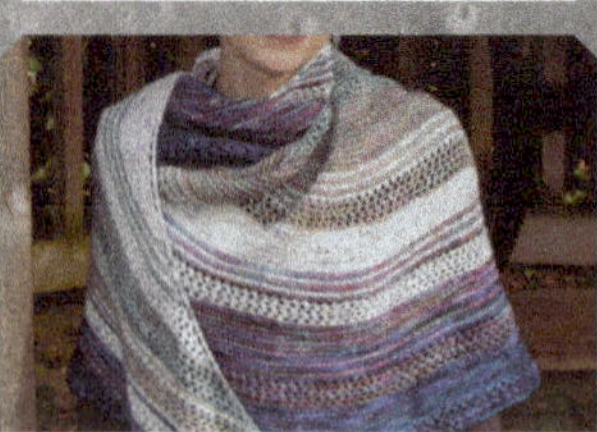

Moontide   45

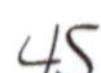

Introduction

For time immemorial, people have pondered the Moon, wondering how it stays up in the sky, why it moves against the fixed stars, of what it is made, and where it goes when it sets into the distant horizon. In addition to the stock response of many exasperated parents -- that's just how it is, now stop asking -- over the years humanity has advanced some very interesting answers to these questions.

The ancient Greeks understood the Moon to proceed in a flat arc or ellipse across the sky, being closer to an Earthly observer when directly overhead than when on the horizon. They also hypothesized that the motion of the Moon was powered by horse. Selene, goddess of the Moon, was the daughter of Titans Hyperion and Theia, and the sister of Eos and Helios. Like her brother, the sun god Helios, Selene drove winged horses before a chariot that carried her across the sky, hers of silver and his of gold. When not traversing the heavens, Selene had many adventures with both gods and mortals, some of which were written down by Hesiod, Virgil, Apollonius of Rhodes, and Sappho.

Unlike the Greek concept of the Moon as goddess, ancient Chinese mythology includes a goddess who lives on the Moon. Thousands of years ago, Chang'e drank an elixir of immortality and floated away from her domineering husband, alighting on the Moon. She lives there still, kept company by the Jade Rabbit. When the Moon is full, the Jade Rabbit can be seen on its face, pounding on a mortar to make more elixir for Chang'e. The oriental Harvest Moon Festival is the annual Earthly celebration of the Lady of the Moon. Mooncakes are among the traditional festival offerings to Chang'e.

More recently, some medieval Europeans thought the pockmarked appearance of the Moon resembled the uneven, lumpy texture of young or fresh cheese. In that era, underripe things of all kinds were referred to as green. Even at the time, the nascent scientific movement within the European Renaissance dismissed out of hand the hypothesis that the Moon is made of green cheese, instead laying down the observational basis for the current working theory of the Moon.

The general inquiry into the Moon continued over the centuries. In 1902, the French illusionist Georges Méliès drew from the works of Jules Verne and produced the seminal silent film A Trip to the Moon. The film features astronomers who travel in a space capsule shot from a giant cannon. After adventures on the Moon with the Roman Moon goddess Phoebe, and with Selenite people living there, the astronomers return to Earth with a captive Selenite. The film was an international sensation.

Then in 1969, in a case of life imitating art, NASA sent astronauts to visit the Moon. While the Apollo 11 rocket was on its way, mission control in Houston, Texas relayed to the crew a news headline to "watch out for a lovely girl with a big rabbit" who had been living on the Moon for 4,000 years. Michael Collins replied from the command module "Ok, we'll keep a close eye out for the bunny girl." However, the astronauts did not find the Jade Rabbit, or winged horses and chariot, or Chang'e, Selene, Phoebe, or any other goddess or denizen of the Moon. They found arid, airless rocks and dust, barren and devoid of life.

Nevertheless, depictions of the Moon as a habitable place, sometimes made of cheese, persist in popular culture, such as in the Aardman Animations short film A Grand Day Out. In this adventure chronicle, Wallace and Gromit experience a severe cheese shortage in their pantry. They resolve their cheese deficit by journeying in a homebuilt rocket from their abode in the north of England to holiday on the Moon. Once there, Wallace samples the local terrain, comparing it to Wensleydale. Gromit disagrees.

Whether one holds with the overwhelming observational and physical evidence that the Moon is a desolate, airless, barren rock, continually orbiting in dynamic balance between hurtling away into space and crashing into the Earth, or one believes in various ancient and contemporary myths about the Moon, the beauty and splendor of the Moon are undimmed through the ages.

About the Knitting

Crescent shawls start with just a few stitches cast on at the center top. All of the shaping increases are worked at the beginning and the end of each row, leaving the uninterrupted center available for lovely stitch patterns and creative color changes. As the shawl grows and can no longer be completely spread out on the needle, keeping track of the final shape can become difficult. Keep in mind as you're working that the increases at each row end are actually forming the top edge of the shawl.

Crescent shawls are versatile and easy to wear. The curved shape allows the shawl to wrap securely around the shoulders without slipping. The long, relatively slender shape of many crescent shawls makes them comfortable to wear wrapped around the neck like a scarf. However you choose to style your shawls, the patterns in this book will allow you to create fun, unique pieces that I hope you will enjoy wearing for years to come.

Binding Off

The outer edge of each crescent shawl needs to expand quite a bit during blocking to form the proper shape. To accommodate this expansion, I recommend the following bind off.

Stretchy Bind Off:
K2, insert the tip of the LH needle into the front of the 2 sts on the RH needle, knit the 2 together through the back loops, *k1, insert the tip of the LH needle into the front of the 2 sts on the RH needle, knit the 2 together through the back loops, rep from * until all sts are bound off.

Yarn

The patterns in this collection are put together such that if you choose your colors carefully, you can knit the seventh shawl, Moontide, using the leftovers from the other six shawls! Please do note that if you decide to increase the size of any of the shawls, or knit at a different gauge than indicated in the book, you may not have enough yarn left to complete the Moontide pattern.

Thank you to Dream in Color for providing all the yarn for this collection. Their "Smooshy" fingering weight yarn comes in a wonderful array of rich colors. It has excellent stitch definition and softens beautifully when blocked. It was a dream to work with.

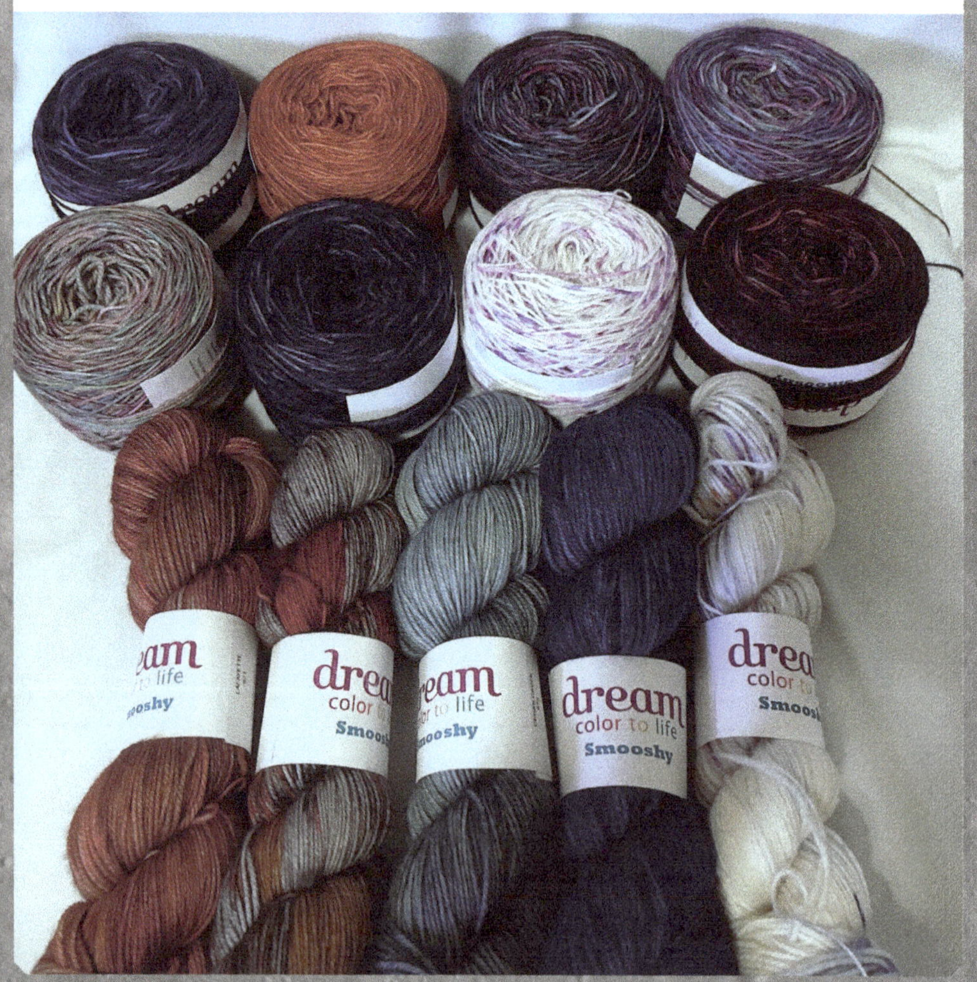

Abbreviations

BO	bind off
brk	brioche knit
brp	brioche purl
cdd	central double decrease
CO	cast on
k	knit
k2tog	knit 2 together
kfbf	knit front back front
kyok	knit yarn over knit (all in one st)
LH	left hand
lp	long purl
m1	make 1
p	purl
p2tog	purl 2 together
p2togtbl	purl two sts together through the back loops
p9tog	purl 9 sts together
pm	place marker
rep	repeat
RH	right hand
RS	right side
sl	slip
sl1yo	slip 1 yarn over
slm	slip marker
ssk	slip slip knit
ssp	slip slip purl
st(s)	stitch(es)
WS	wrong side
yo	yarn over

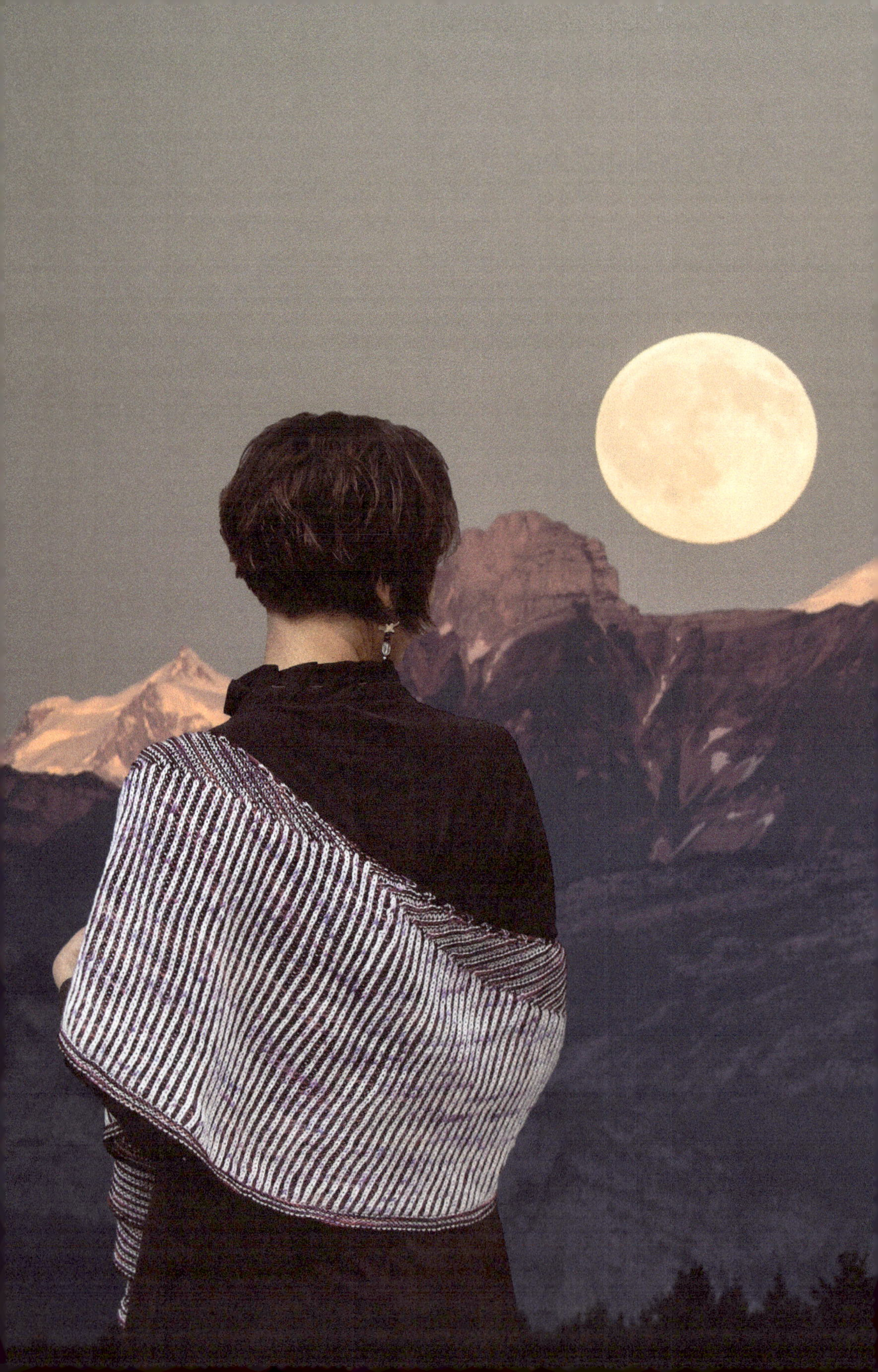

Moonrise

Brioche and garter stitch combine in this shawl to create vertical and horizontal stripes. The pattern includes instructions for the brioche stitches and is suitable for someone who has not knit brioche before. This is a great project for playing with color and texture.

FINISHED MEASUREMENTS
Wingspan: 70 inches / 178 cm
Depth: 14 inches / 35.5 cm
Size is easily adjustable by using more or less yarn.

MATERIALS
Yarn: Two contrasting colors of fingering weight yarn.
Shown in Dream in Color Smooshy; 85% superwash fine merino wool, 15% nylon; 420 yards/4 ounces
Color A: Concord, 390 yards
Color B: Still I Rise, 370 yards

Needles: 40 inch US #5 / 3.75 mm circular needle, or size needed to obtain gauge

Tapestry needle

GAUGE
25 sts = 4 inches / 10 cm in garter stitch

SPECIAL STITCHES
Brk (brioche knit): Knit the stitch together with its yarn over

Brp (brioche purl): Kurl the stitch together with its yarn over

Kyok (knit, yarn over, knit): Knit, then yo, then knit again into the same stitch. Three sts made from 1 st.

Sl1yo (slip 1 yarn over): With the yarn in front, slip the stitch purlwise and bring the yarn over the needle. The slipped stitch with its yo are considered one stitch.

Pattern

Set-Up

With color A

CO 7 sts.

Row 1: Knit.

Row 2: K2, yo, k3, yo, k2.

Row 3: K2, kyok, k3, kyok, k2.

Row 4: K2, yo, k9, yo, k2.

Row 5: K2, kyok, k9, kyok, k2.

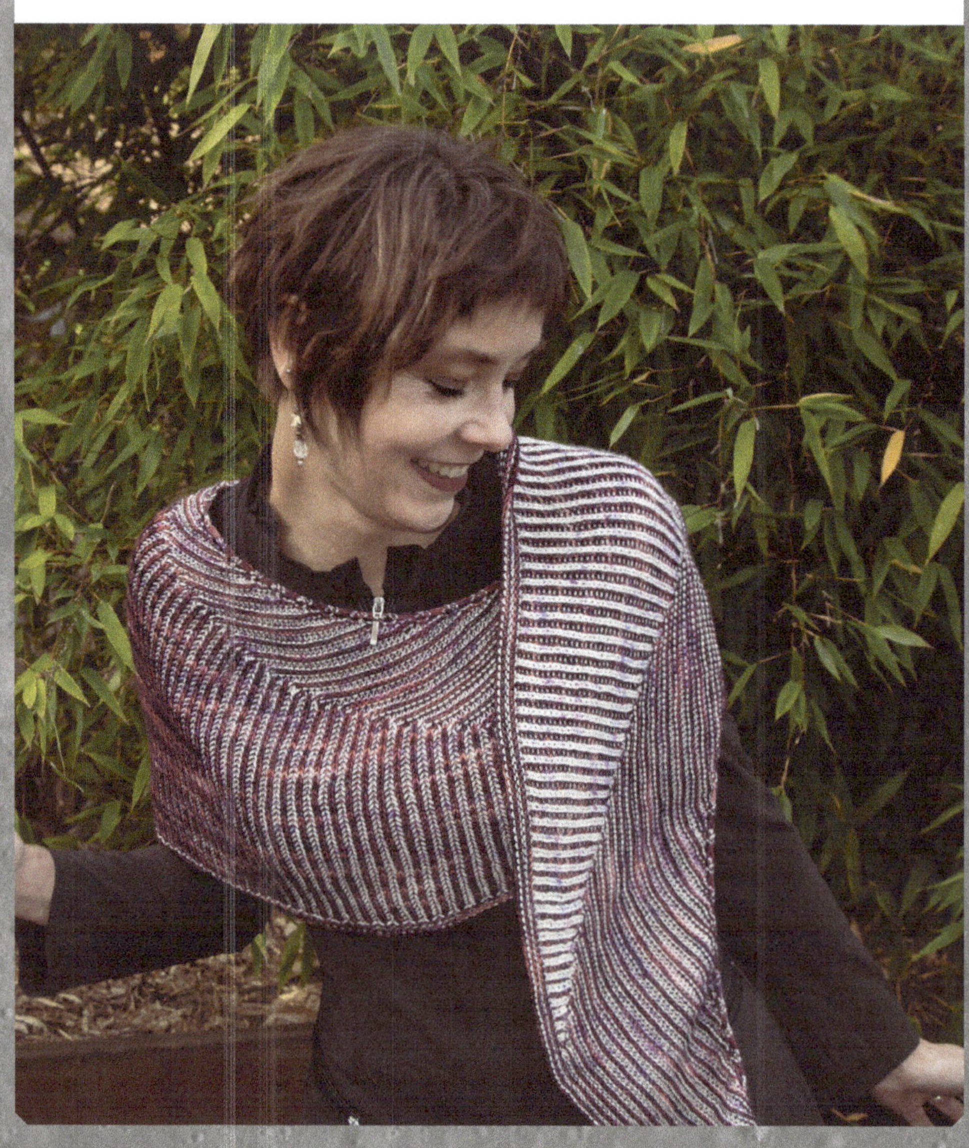

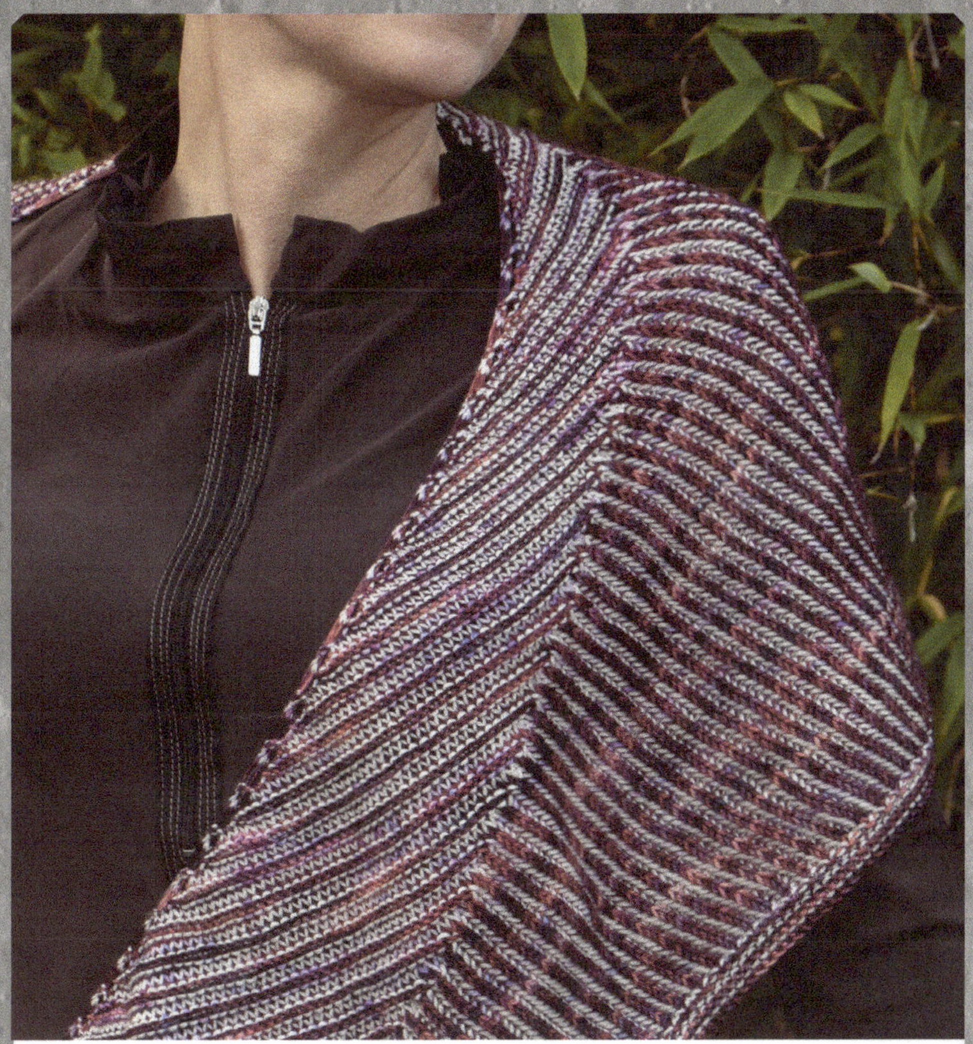

Switch to color B
Row 6: K2, yo, k6, p1, sl1yo, p1, k6, yo, k2.
Push the stitches back to LH tip of the needle and work the next row on the same side of the work as the previous row.
Switch to color A
Row 7: K2, kyok, k6, sl1yo, brk1, sl1yo, k6, kyok, k2.

Body
Switch to color B
Row 8: K2, yo, knit to 1 st before the first sl1yo from the previous row, *sl1yo, brk1, rep from * until you have worked the last brioche st from the previous row, sl1yo, knit to last 2 sts, yo, k2.

Push the stitches back to LH tip of the needle and work the next row on the same side of the work as the previous row.
Switch to color A
Row 9: K2, kyok, knit to 1 st before the first sl1yo from the previous row, *sl1yo, brp1, rep from * to last brioche st, sl1yo, knit to last 3 sts, kyok, k2.
Switch to color B
Row 10: K2, yo, knit to 1 st before the first sl1yo from the previous row, *sl1yo, brp1, rep from * until you have worked the last brioche st from the previous row, sl1yo, knit to last 2 sts, yo, k2.
Push the stitches back to LH tip of the needle and work the next row on the same side of the work as the previous row.
Switch to color A
Row 11: K2, kyok, knit to 1 st before the first sl1yo from the previous row, *sl1yo, brk1, rep from * to last brioche st, sl1yo, knit to last 3 sts, kyok, k2.
Rep rows 8 - 11 until you've used most of the yarn or the shawl is the desired size. Be sure there is at least 15 gm of color A and 12 gm of color B left.

Edge
Switch to color B
Row 12: K2, yo, knit to last 2 sts (use brk for all brioche sts that include a yarn over), yo, k2. Push the stitches back to LH tip of the needle and work the next row on the same side of the work as the previous row.
Switch to color A
Row 13: K2, kyok, knit to last 3 sts, kyok, k2.
Rep rows 12 and 13 three more times.
With color A, BO all sts using the stretchy bind off on pg 7.
Block gently, creating the crescent shape.

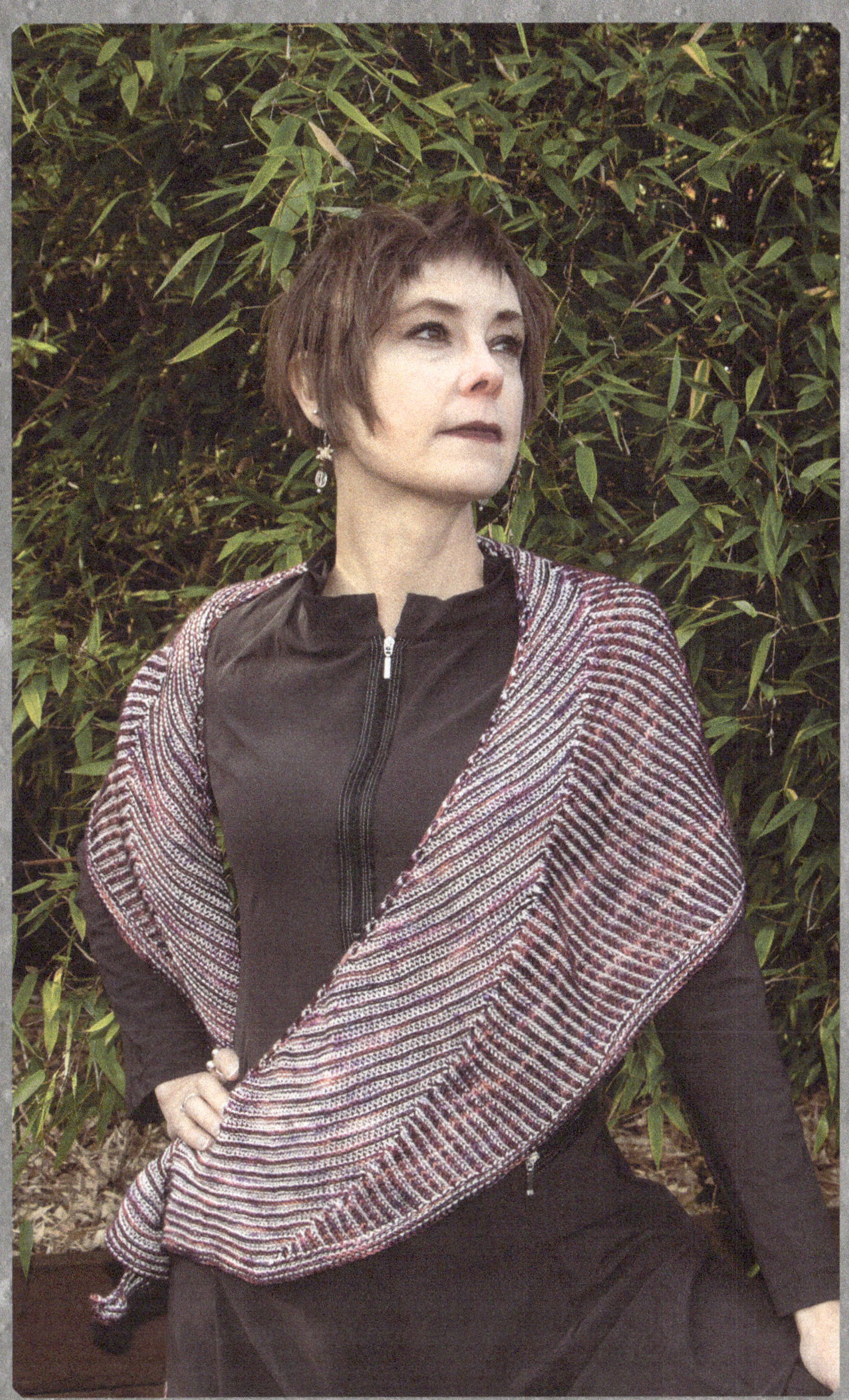
Moonrise 15

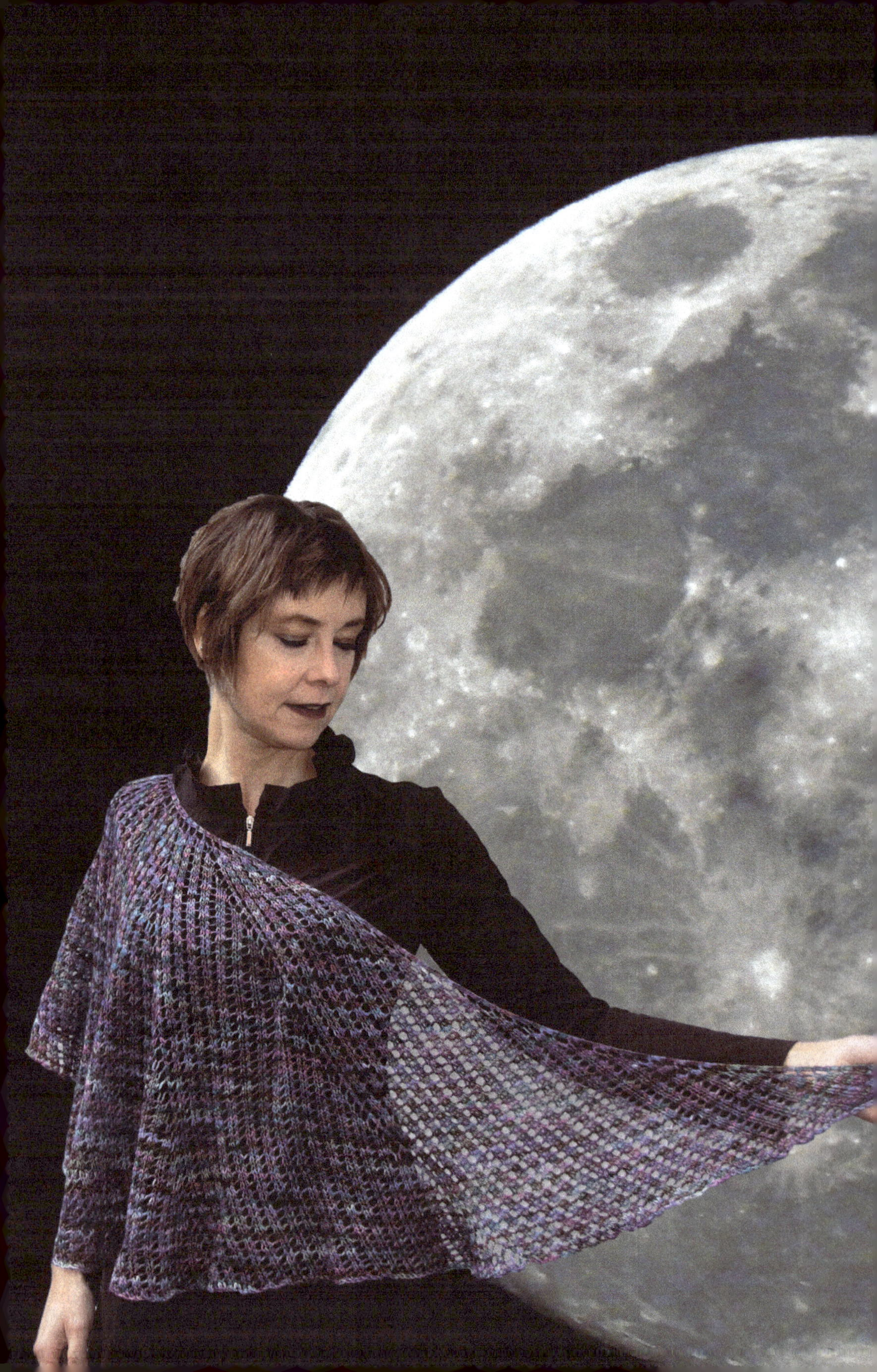

Moonbeams

The shawl has both standard crescent shaping and increases within each lace section. The result is a spiral shape that sits very securely around the shoulders. The lace pattern looks complex but is simple enough to memorize.

Finished Measurements
Wingspan: 54 inches / 137 cm
Depth: 17 inches / 43 cm
Size is easily adjustable by using more or less yarn.

Materials
Yarn: One color of fingering weight yarn.
Shown in Dream in Color Smooshy; 85% superwash fine merino wool, 15% nylon; 420 yards/4 ounces
Color: My Fair Lady, 560 yards

Needles: 40 inch US #6 / 4 mm circular needle, or size needed to obtain gauge

14 stitch markers
Tapestry needle

Gauge
23 sts = 4 inches / 10 cm in the following lace pattern:
CO a mult of 4 sts.
Row 1: *Ssk, yo, k1, rep from * to end of row.
Row 2: Purl.
Rep rows 1 and 2 until swatch is large enough.

Special Stitches
Kyok (knit, yarn over, knit): Knit, then yo, then knit again into the same stitch. Three sts made from 1 st.

A section is defined as the set of sts between two markers. This does not include the sts before the first marker or after the last marker.

Pattern
CO 4 sts.
Set Up
Row 1 (RS): K4.
Row 2 (WS): K2, pm, yo, k2.
Row 3: K2, kyok, slm, k2.

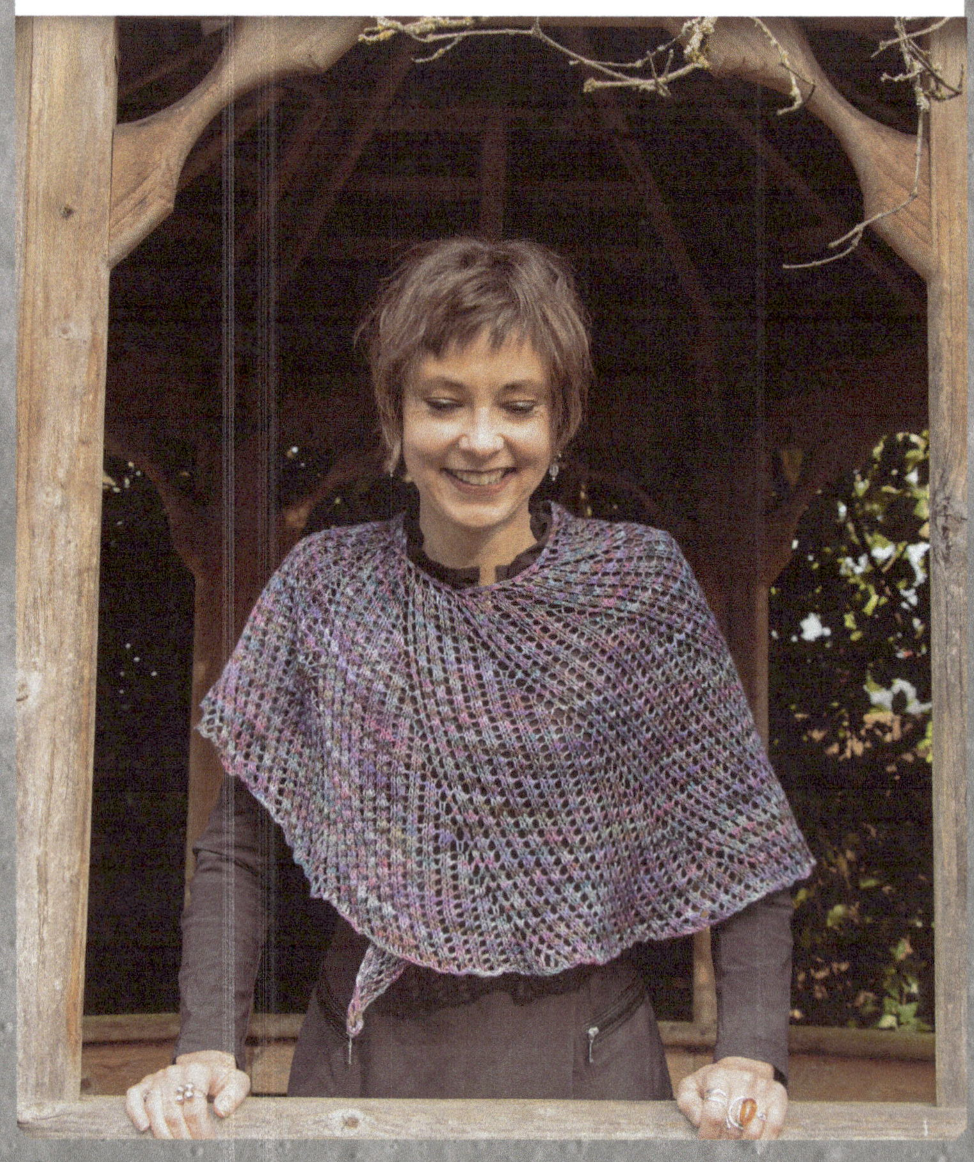

Row 4: K2, slm, p3, yo, k2.
Row 5: K2, kyok, ssk, yo, k1, yo, slm, k2.
Row 6: K2, slm, p7, yo, k2.
Row 7: K2, kyok, [ssk, yo, k1] twice, k1, yo, slm, k2.
Row 8: K2, slm, p11, yo, k2.
Row 9: K2, kyok, [ssk, yo, k1] three times, k2, yo, slm, k2.

Body
Row 10: K2, purl to last 2 sts (slipping all markers as you come to them), pm, yo, k2.
Row 11: K2, kyok, slm, [*ssk, yo, k1, rep from * until 0, 1, or 2 sts remain in the section, k to marker, yo, slm] rep for all remaining sections, k2.

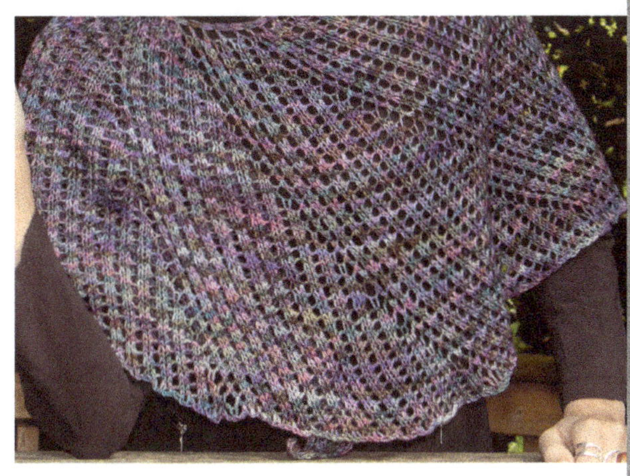

Rows 12, 14, and 16: K2, purl to last 2 sts (slipping all markers as you come to them), yo, k2.
Row 13: K2, kyok, ssk, yo, k1, yo, slm, [*ssk, yo, k1, rep from * until 0, 1, or 2 sts remain in the section, k to marker, yo, slm] rep for all remaining sections, k2.
Row 15: K2, kyok, [ssk, yo, k1] twice, k1, yo, slm, [*ssk, yo, k1, rep from * until 0, 1, or 2 sts remain in the section, k to marker, yo, slm] rep for all remaining sections, k2.
Row 17: K2, kyok, [ssk, yo, k1] three times, k2, yo, slm, [*ssk, yo, k1, rep from * until 0, 1, or 2 sts remain in the section, k to marker, yo, slm] rep for all remaining sections, k2.
Rep rows 10 - 17 until you have 14 markers on the needle.
BO all sts using the stretchy bind off on pg 7.
Block somewhat aggressively to open the lace and create the spiral shape.

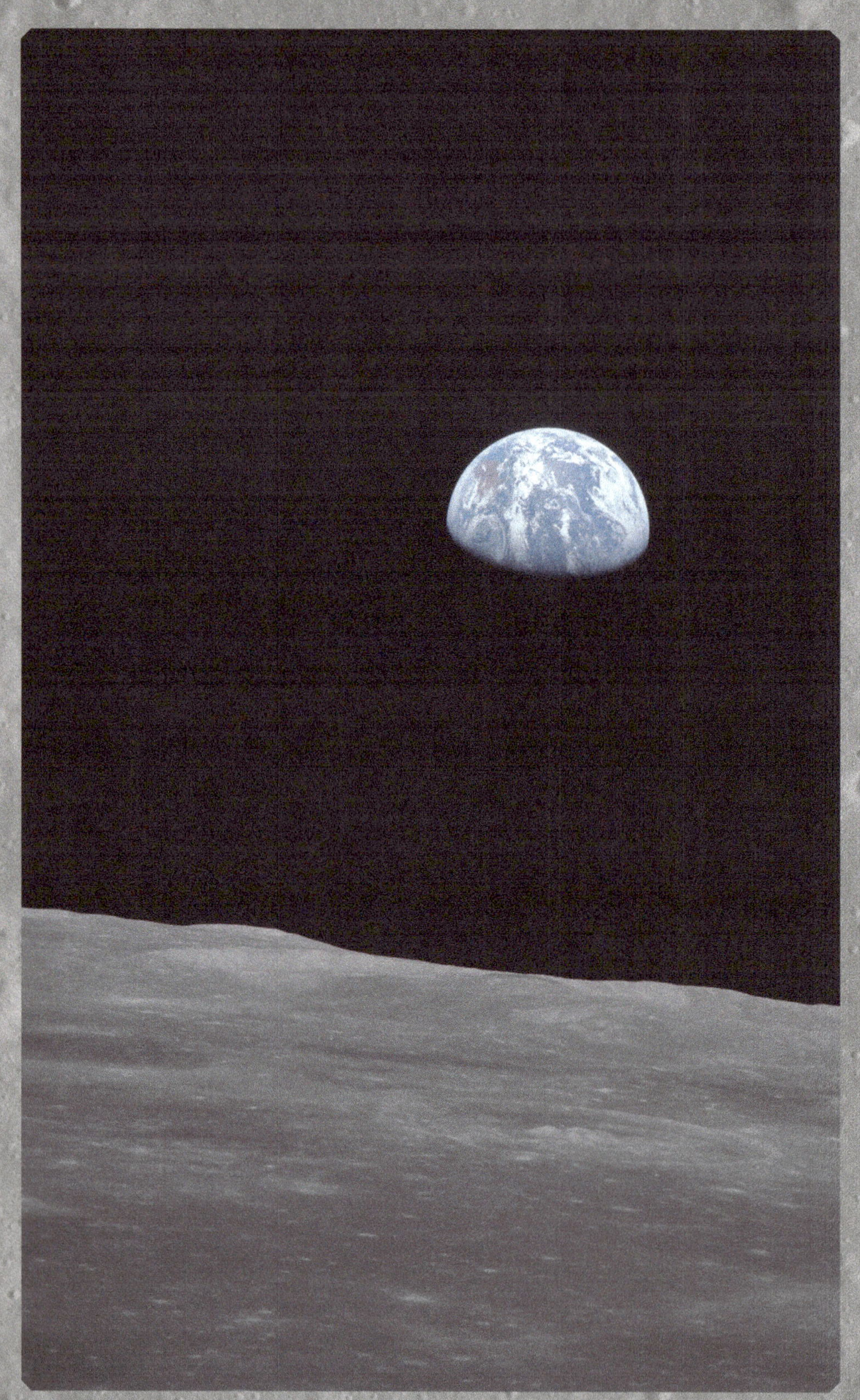

20 Crescents

Earthrise: the photo that launched a movement

On December 24th, 1968, astronaut William Anders took a photo of Earth out the window of the Apollo 8 command module while in orbit around the moon. Apollo 8 was the first manned mission to orbit the moon, though they would not land on the moon. The objective of the mission was to test equipment and procedures and to photograph prospective landing sites for future missions, paving the way for the successful landing of Apollo 11.

But perhaps more important in the long run than the reconnaissance was that photo Anders snapped out the window. The crew had a list of photos to take and this one wasn't on it. But when they saw the earth rising above the surface of the moon they agreed that they would take the picture anyway. The photo, later dubbed "Earthrise," was the first time that we saw the entirety of our own planet. It showed us how delicate, how isolated, and how exquisitely beautiful our home is.

The publication of the Earthrise photo drove home the idea that the planet is finite and alerted us to its lonely fragility. Seeing that beautiful marbled blue jewel floating alone in the void of space sparked conversations about protecting the one home we have. The photo is often cited at the starting point of the environmental movement. In the years since, Earthrise has become part of our collective consciousness. In 2003, Earthrise was on the cover of Life's 100 Photographs that Changed the World.

"We set out to explore the moon and instead discovered the Earth."

-William Anders

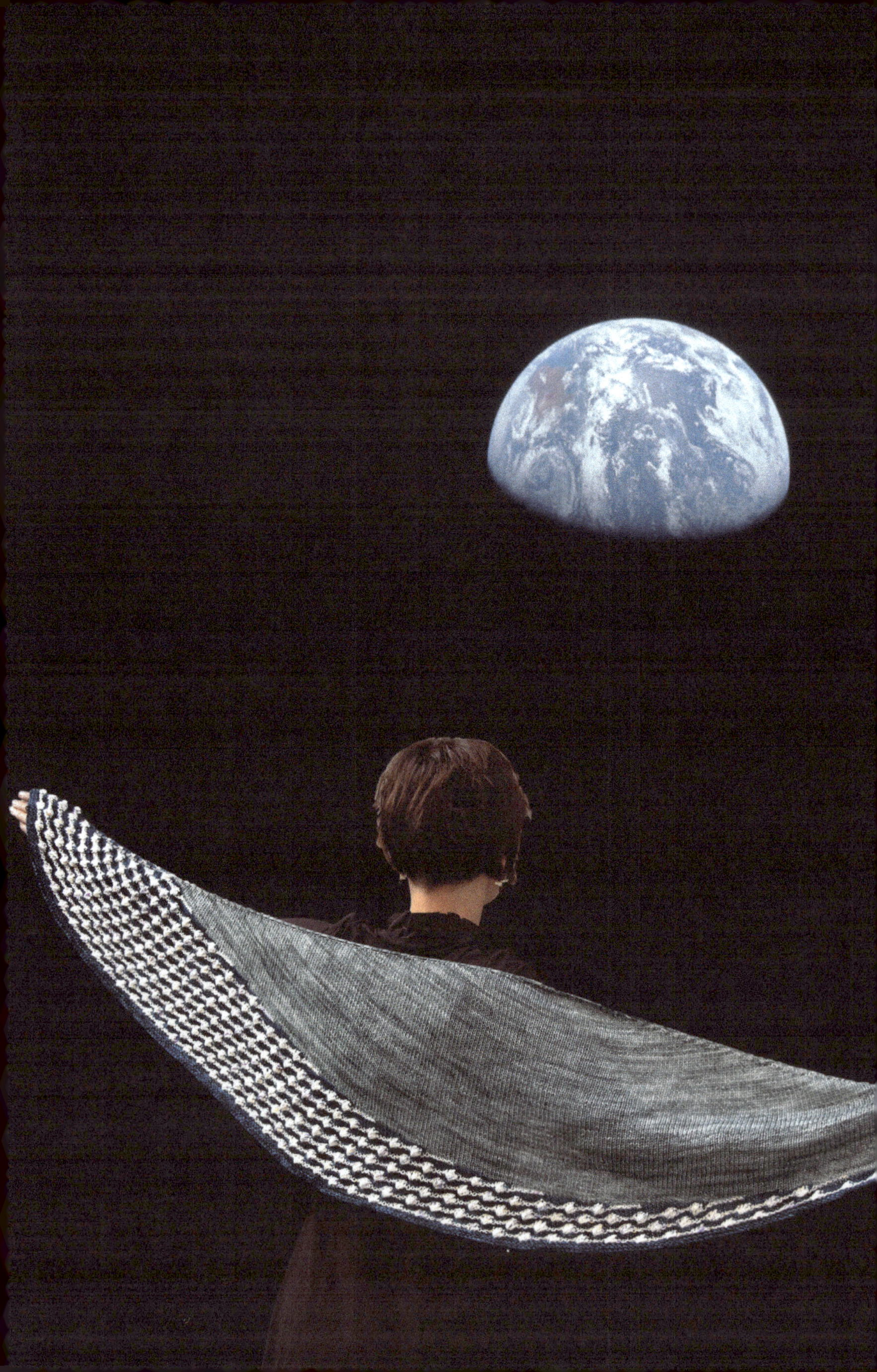

Earthrise

A lovely stockinette stitch crescent is wrapped in a heavily textured, asymmetrical edging. The heavy texture of the edge creates visual interest and drama.

FINISHED MEASUREMENTS
Wingspan: 72 inches / 183 cm
Depth: 15 inches / 38 cm

MATERIALS
Yarn: Three colors of fingering weight yarn.
Shown in Dream in Color Smooshy; 85% superwash fine merino wool, 15% nylon; 420 yards/4 ounces
Color A: Cedar Creek, 300 yards
Color B: Blue Fish, 200 yards
Color C: Whisper, 200 yards

Needles : 40 inch US #6 / 4 mm circular needle, or size needed to obtain gauge

Tapestry needle

GAUGE
18 sts = 4 inches / 10 cm in stockinette stitch

SPECIAL STITCHES
Kfbf (knit front back front): Knit into the front, then the back, and then the front of 1 sts. Three sts made from one st.

Kyok (knit, yarn over, knit): Knit, then yo, then knit again into the same stitch. Three sts made from 1 st.

Lp (long purl): Purl the stitch, wrapping the yarn around the needle twice.

M1 (make one): Lift the bar between sts with the LH needle from front to back then knit into the back loop. This will twist the bar and create a new st without leaving a hole.

Pattern
Moon
With color A, CO 8 sts.
Row 1 (WS): Knit.
Row 2 (RS): Knit.
Row 3: K2, yo, k4, yo, k2.
Row 4: K2, kyok, k4, kyok, k2.
Row 5: K2, yo, k10, yo, k2.
Row 6: K2, kyok, knit to last 3 sts, kyok, k2.
Row 7: K2, yo, purl to last 2 sts, yo, k2.
Rep rows 6 and 7 until there are 92 yos along the top edge (280 sts) and cut color A.

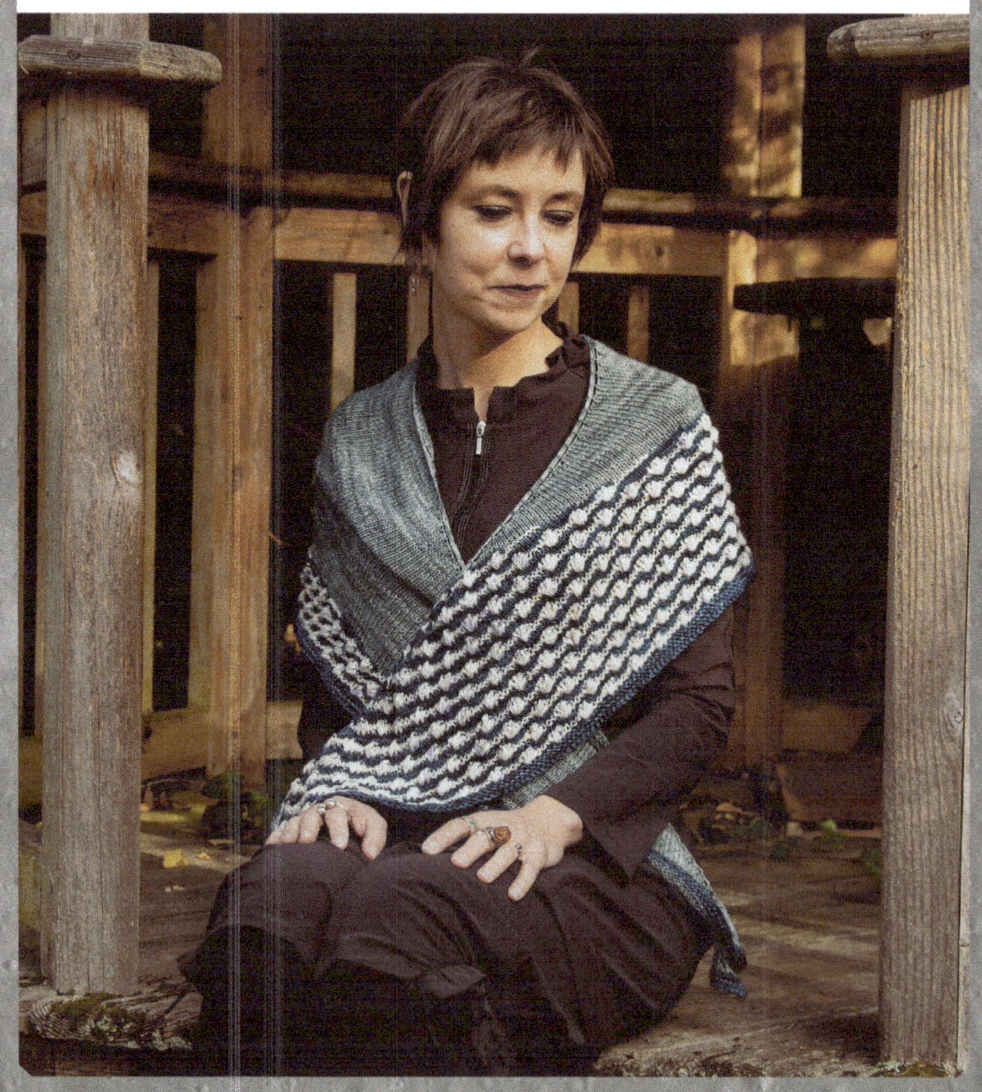

Earth

Switch to color B

Row 8: K2, kyok, k7, turn.

Row 9: Yo, p10, yo, k2.

Switch to color C (leave color B attached.)

Row 10: K2, kyok, kfbf, kfbf, kfbf, k3, kfbf, kfbf, kfbf, k1, k2tog, k6, turn.

Row 11: Yo, k8, [lp9, k3] twice, yo, k2.

Switch to color B (leave color C attached.)

Row 12: K2, kyok, [k3, sl9 dropping the extra loops] twice, k8, k2tog, k6, turn.

Row 13: Yo, p14, [m1, p1, p9tog, p1, m1, p1] twice, p4, yo, k2.

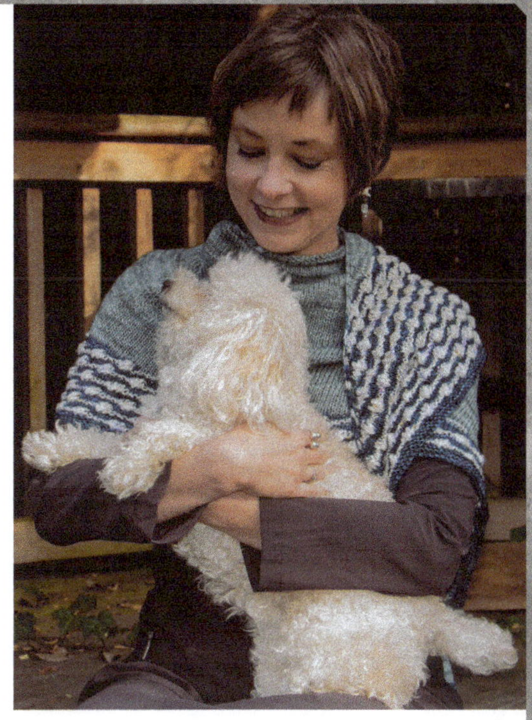

Row 14: K2, kyok, knit to yo from the previous row, k2tog, k6, turn.

Row 15: Yo, purl to last 2 sts, yo, k2.

Switch to color C (leave color B attached.)

Row 16: K2, kyok, kfbf, kfbf, kfbf, *k3, kfbf, kfbf, kfbf, rep from * to last 2 color B sts, k1, k2tog, k6, turn.

Row 17: Yo, k8, *lp9, k3, rep from * to last 2 sts, yo, k2.

Switch to color B (leave color C attached.)

Row 18: K2, kyok, *k3, sl9 dropping the extra loops, rep from * to last 9 color C sts, k8, k2tog, k6, turn.

Row 19: Yo, p14, *m1, p1, p9tog, p1, m1, p1, rep from * to last 6 sts, p4, yo, k2.

Rep rows 14 - 19 nine more times (ten reps total.)

Row 20: K2, kyok, knit to yo from the previous row, k2tog, knit to last 3 sts, kyok, k2.

Row 21: K2, yo, purl to last 2 sts, yo, k2.

Row 22: K2, kyok, knit to last 3 sts, kyok, k2.

Rep rows 21 and 22 once more.

BO all sts using the stretchy bind off on page 7.

Block gently, creating the crescent shape.

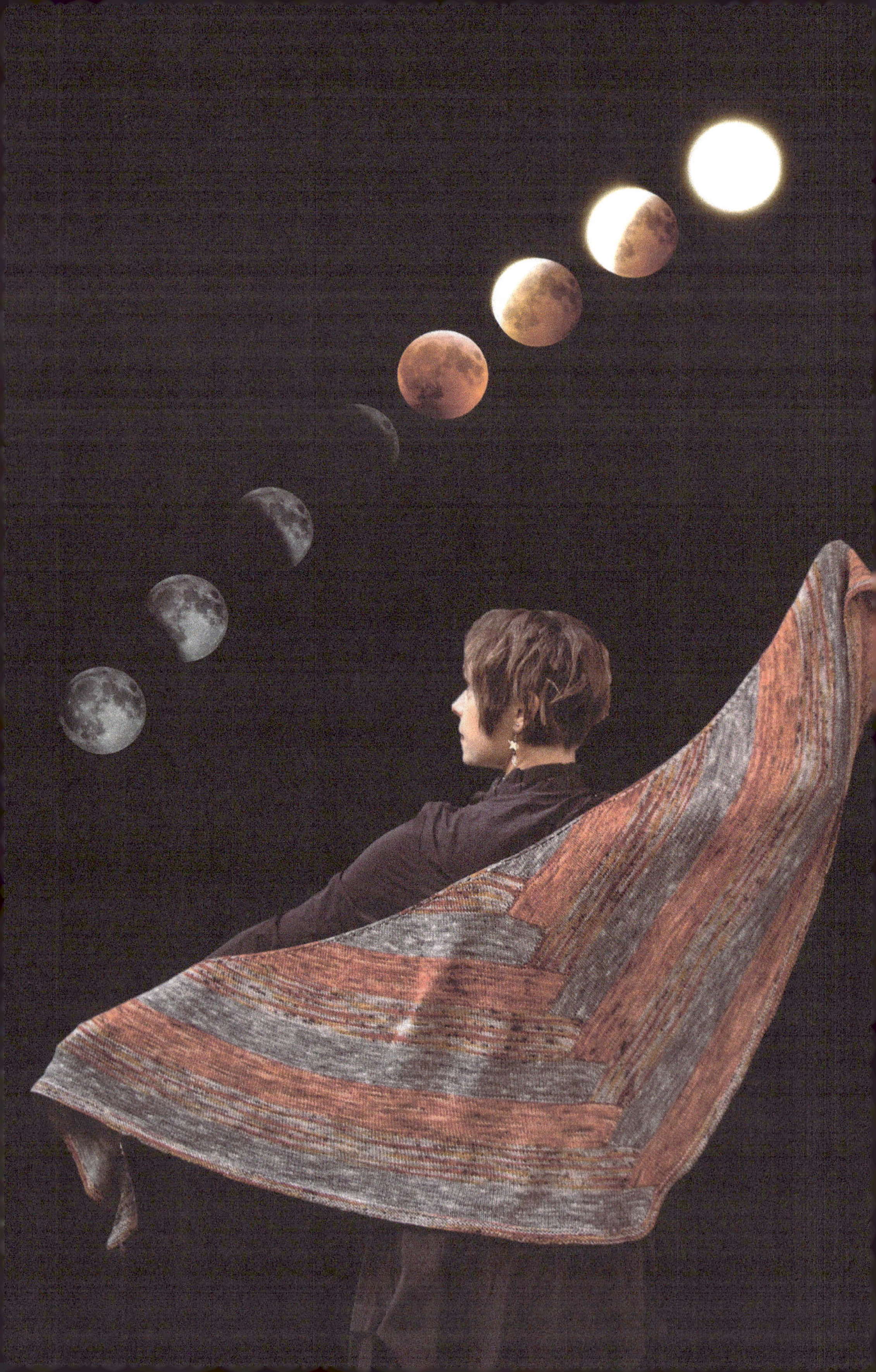

Eclipse

This shawl is knit in alternating left and right side strips with stitches picked up along the selvedge edge of the previous strip. The result is a more traditional triangular shawl with a curved upper edge.

Finished Measurements
Wingspan: 92 inches / 234 cm
Depth: 22 inches / 56 cm

Materials
Yarn: Three colors of fingering weight yarn.
Shown in Dream in Color Smooshy; 85% superwash fine merino wool, 15% nylon; 420 yards/4 ounces
Color A: Prince William, 285 yards
Color B: Cloud to Ground, 360 yards
Color C: Lafayette, 285 yards

Needles: 40 inch US #5 / 3.75 mm circular needle, or size needed to obtain gauge

Tapestry needle

Gauge
20 sts = 4 inches / 10 cm in stockinette stitch

Special Stitches
Kyok (knit, yarn over, knit): Knit, then yo, then knit again into the same stitch. Three sts made from 1 st.

PATTERN NOTES
You will rotate through the three different colored yarns in set order
(always A, then B, then C.) When the pattern says to start the next
color be sure to stay in order.
As written, you will work the edge and bind off with yarn B. Adding
or subtracting stripes may change which yarn is used at the edge and
you would need to adjust yarn amounts accordingly.

PATTERN
Set Up
First Right Side Stripe
With color A, CO 4 sts
Row 1 (RS): K4.
Row 2 (WS): K2, yo, k2.
Row 3: K2, kyok, k2.
Row 4: K2, yo, k5.
Row 5: K5, kyok, k2.
Row 6: K2, yo, p6, p2togtbl.
Row 7: Knit to last 3 sts, kyok, k2.
Row 8: K2, yo, purl to last 2 sts, p2togtbl.
Rep rows 7 and 8 six more times. There will be 10 yos along the top
edge of the shawl.

First Left Side Stripe
Switch to color B.
Working a RS row, pick up knitwise 15 sts along the selvedge edge
of the stripe just worked.
Row 9 (WS): Purl to last 2 sts, yo, k2.
Row 10 (RS): K2, kyok, knit to last 2 sts, k2tog.
Rep rows 9 and 10 nine more times. There will be 10 new yos along
the top edge of the shawl.

Body
Right Side Stripe
Switch to next color.
Working a RS row, pick up knitwise 15 sts along the selvedge edge
of the left side stripe just worked. Finish the first RS row by working
the live sts from the previous right side stripe as written in row 11.
Then work row 12 across the live sts from the previous right side
stripe and the picked up sts. DO NOT work the live sts from the left
side stripe just completed.

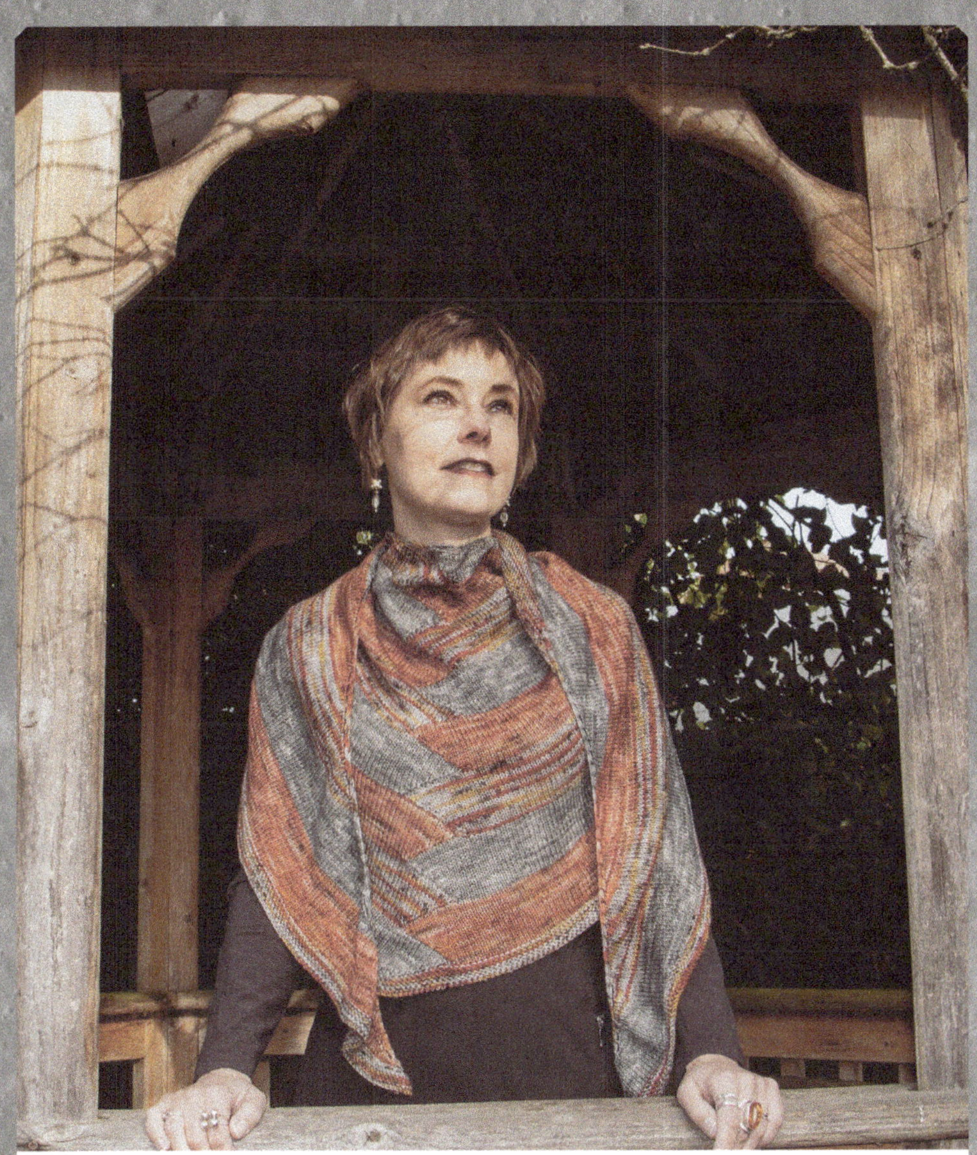

Row 11 (RS): Knit to last 3 sts, kyok, k2.
Row 12 (WS): K2, yo, purl to last 2 sts, p2togtbl.
Rep rows 11 and 12 nine more times. There will be 10 new yos along the top edge of the shawl.

Left Side Stripe
Switch to next color.
Working a WS row, pick up purlwise 15 sts along the selvedge edge of the right side stripe just worked. Finish the first WS row by working the live sts from the previous left side stripe as written in

row 13. Then work row 14 across the live sts from the previous left side stripe and the picked up sts. DO NOT work the live sts from the right side stripe just completed.

Row 13 (WS): Purl to last 2 sts, yo, k2.
Row 14 (RS): K2, kyok, knit to last 2 sts, k2tog.
Rep rows 13 and 14 nine more times. There will be 10 new yos along the top edge of the shawl.

Continue alternating right side and left side stripes until there are 16 stripes total. You can adjust the finished size by adding or subtracting pairs of stripes as desired.

Edge
Switch to next color.
Working a RS row, pick up knitwise 15 sts along the selvedge edge of the left side stripe just worked. Finish the first RS row by working the live sts from the previous right side stripe as written in row 11 above.
Working ALL live sts on the needle:
Row 15 (WS): K2, yo, knit to last 2 sts, yo, k2.
Row 16 (RS): K2, kyok, knit to last 3 sts, kyok, k2.
Rep rows 15 and 16 three more times (four reps total.)
BO all sts using the stretchy bind off on page 7.
Block gently, taking care to shape the point at the center back.

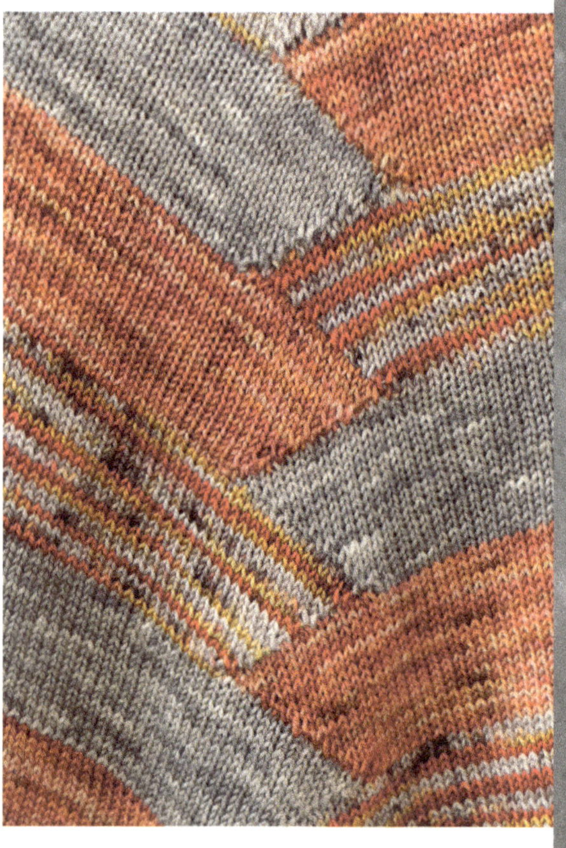

Lunar Eclipse

A lunar eclipse occurs when the earth passes between the sun and the moon, casting its shadow on the moon. Unlike a solar eclipse, a lunar eclipse can be safely watched with the naked eye and requires no special equipment for viewing.

The highlight of a lunar eclipse is the dark orange/red color that the moon takes on during totality. This color is the result of light scattering by the earth's atmosphere. The shorter wavelengths (blues) are scattered while the longer wavelengths (reds) pass through the atmosphere, reaching the moon and bouncing back toward the earth to be perceived by us as a "blood moon."

Throughout history, these mysterious darkenings of the moon have been taken as shows of displeasure by the gods, or as portents of doom. Eclipses influenced the outcomes of wars and other power struggles for thousands of years. But early astronomers worked out the cause of lunar eclipses and were able to predict them with fair accuracy. Savvy leaders used this information to influence the behavior of the uneducated masses and to sway public opinion.

"The Moon in the midst of a clear sky became suddenly eclipsed; the soldiers who were ignorant of the cause took this for an omen referring to their present adventures: to their labors they compared the eclipse of the planet, and prophesied 'that if to the distressed goodness should be restored her wonted brightness and splendor, equally successful would be the issue of their struggle.' Hence they made a loud noise, by ringing upon brazen metal, and by blowing trumpets and cornets; as she appeared brighter or darker they exulted or lamented."

-Tacitus (1st century CE)
writing about an eclipse that
occurred on Sept. 27, 14 CE

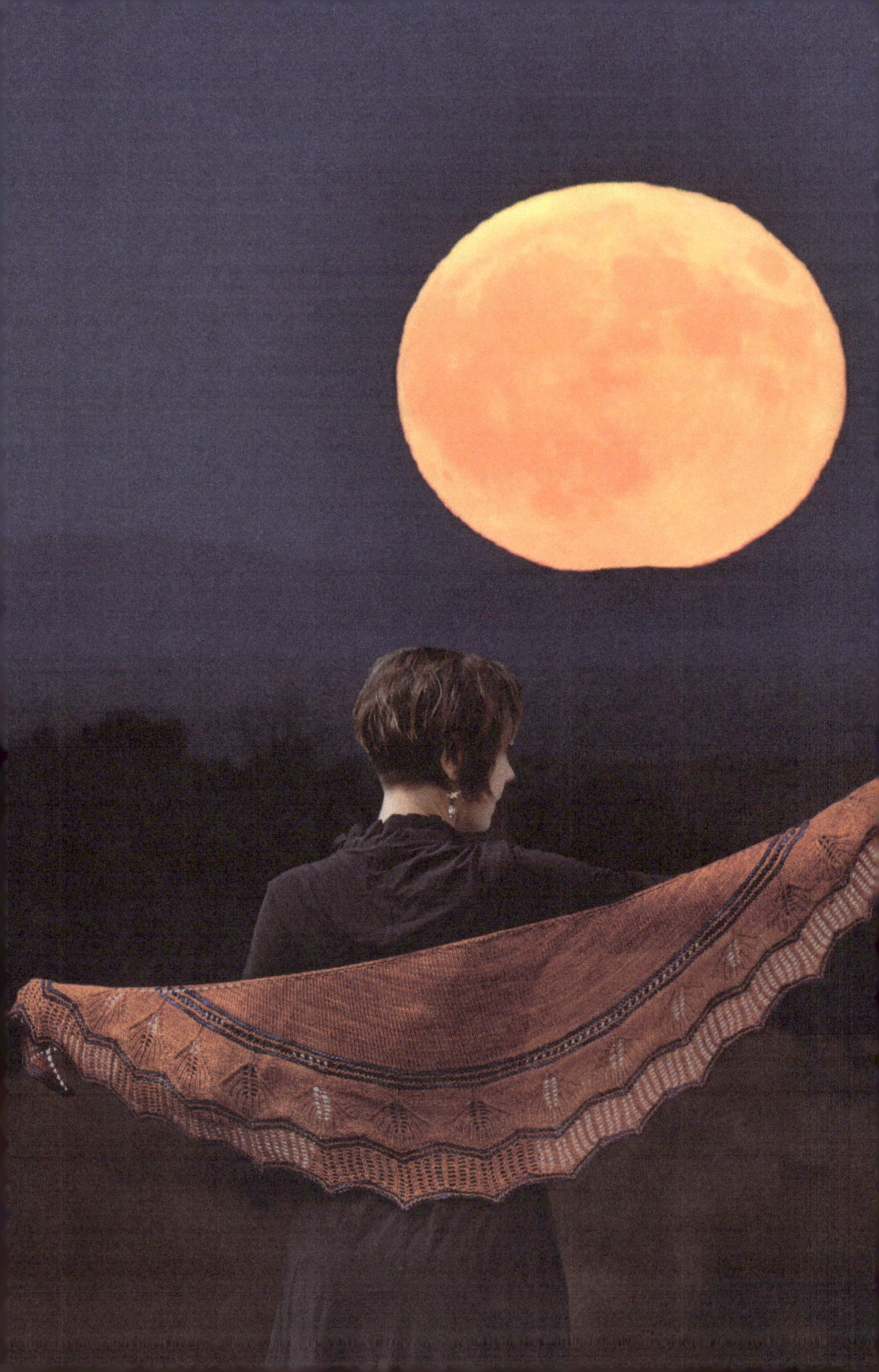

Harvest Moon

The stockinette stitch body of this shawl is wrapped in bands
of delicate lace and contrasting stripes of color. The result is a
traditional, symmetrical crescent shawl.

FINISHED MEASUREMENTS
Wingspan: 68 inches / 173 cm
Depth: 16 inches / 41 cm

MATERIALS
Yarn: Two colors of fingering weight yarn.
Shown in Dream in Color Smooshy; 85% superwash fine merino
wool, 15% nylon; 420 yards/4 ounces
Color A: Tex Mex, 310 yards
Color B: Elysian, 70 yards

Needles: 40 inch US #5 / 3.75 mm circular needle, or size needed to
obtain gauge

Stitch Markers
Tapestry needle

GAUGE
20 sts = 4 inches / 10 cm in stockinette stitch

SPECIAL STITCHES
Cdd (central double decrease): Slip 2 sts together knitwise, k1, pass
slipped sts over the knit st.

Kyok (knit, yarn over, knit): Knit, then yo, then knit again into the
same stitch. Three sts made from 1 st.

M1 (make one): Lift the bar between sts with the LH needle from
front to back then knit into the back loop. This will twist the bar and
create a new st without leaving a hole.

PATTERN

With color A, CO 7 sts.
Row 1 (RS): knit.
Row 2 (WS): K2, yo, k3, yo, k2.
Row 3: K2, kyok, k3, kyok, k2.
Row 4: K2, yo, k9, yo, k2.
Row 5: K2, kyok, knit to last 3 sts, kyok, k2.
Row 6: K2, yo, purl to last 2 sts, yo, k2.
Rep rows 5 and 6 until there are 60 yos along the top edge (183 sts)
Switch to color B leaving color A attached.
Row 7: K2, kyok, knit to last 3 sts, kyok, k2.
Row 8: K2, yo, knit to last 2 sts, yo, k2.
Switch to color A leaving color B attached.
Rep rows 7 and 8 once.
Switch to color B leaving color A attached.
Row 9: K2, kyok, knit to last 3 sts, kyok, k2.
Row 10: K2, yo, *p2tog, yo, rep from * to last 3 sts, p1, yo, k2.
Switch to color A leaving color B attached.
Rep rows 7 and 8 once.
Switch to color B leaving color A attached.
Rep rows 7 and 8 once.
You will now have 70 yos along the top edge (213 sts).

Wheat Section
Switch to color A. Either carry the color B along the edge, wrapping the yarns every other row, or cut the color B and reattach it later.
Row 11: K2, kyok, knit to last 3 sts, kyok, k2.
Row 12: K2, yo, k7, *p1, k17, rep from * to last 10 sts, p1, k7, yo, k2.
Row 13: K2, kyok, p7, *k1, p17, rep from * to last 11 sts, k1, p7, kyok, k2.
Row 14: K2, yo, k10, *p1, k17, rep from * to last 13 sts, p1, k10, yo, k2.
Row 15: K2, kyok, p1, pm, p1, *p8, k1, p9, rep from * to last 4 sts, pm, p1, kyok, k2.
You will now have 74 yos along the top edge (229 sts).
Row 16: K2, yo, k4, slm, *k9, p1, k8, rep from * to 1 st before marker, k1, slm, k4, yo, k2.
Row 17: K2, kyok, p4, slm, p1, *p7, k3, p8, rep from * to marker, slm, p4, kyok, k2.
Row 18: K2, yo, k7, slm, *k8, p3, k7, rep from * to 1 st before marker, k1, slm, k7, yo, k2.

Row 19: K2, kyok, p7, slm, p1 *p6, k2tog, yo, k1, yo, ssk, p7, rep from * to marker, slm, p7, kyok, k2.
Row 20: K2, yo, p4, k6, slm, *k7, p5, k6, rep from * to 1 st before marker, k1, slm, k7, p3, yo, k2.
Row 21: K2, kyok, k1, yo, p1, ssk, p6, slm, p1, *p5, k2tog, p1, yo, k1, yo, p1, ssk, p6, rep from * to marker, slm, p5, k2tog, p1, yo, k2, kyok, k2.

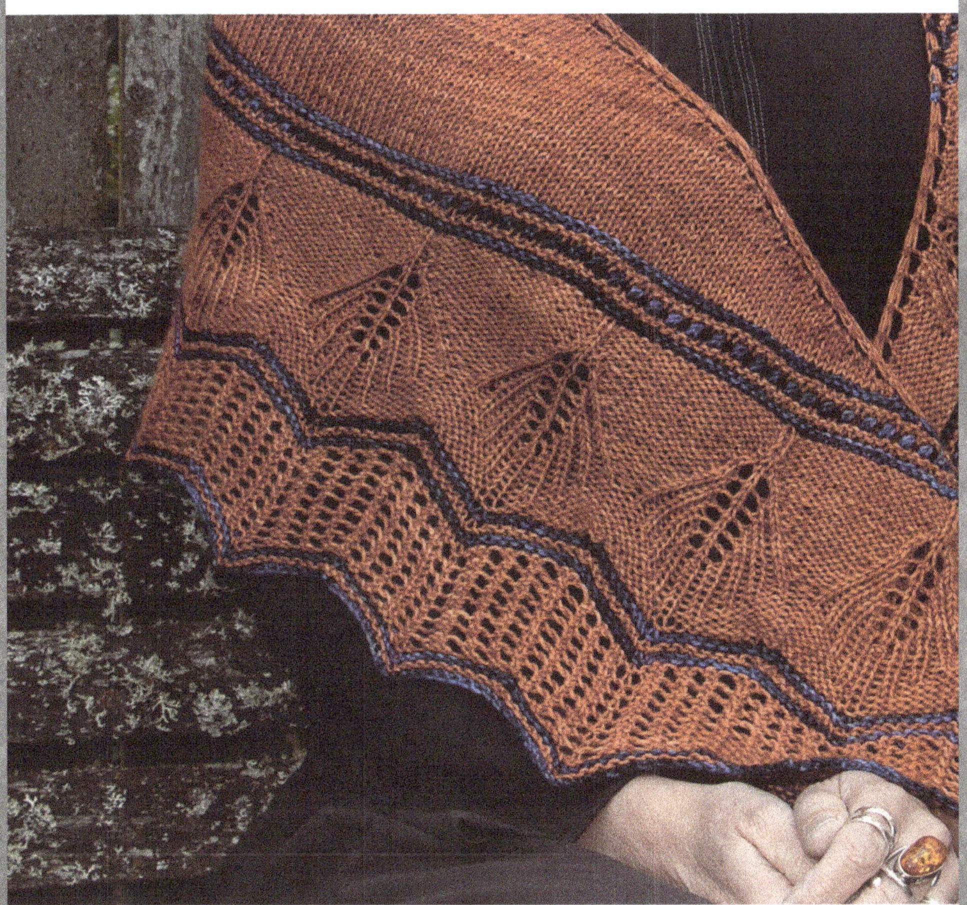

Row 22: K2, yo, p2, k1, p3, k1, p1, k5, slm, *k6, p1, k1, p3, k1, p1, k5, rep from * to 1 st before marker, k1, slm, k6, p1, k1, p3, k2, yo, k2.
Row 23: K2, kyok, p1, k3, yo, k1, p1, ssk, p5, slm, p1,* p4, k2tog, p1, k1, yo, k1, yo, k1, p1, ssk, p5, rep from * to marker, slm, p4, k2tog, p1, k1, yo, k1, yo, k1, p1, ssk, kyok, k2.
Row 24: K2, yo, k3, p1, k1, p5, k1, p1, k4, slm, *k5, p1, k1, p5, k1, p1, k4, rep from * to 1 st before marker, k1, slm, k5, p1, k1, p5, k1, p1, k2, yo, k2.

Row 25: K2, kyok, p1, k2tog, p1, k1, p1, yo, k1, yo, p1, k1, p1, ssk, p4, remove marker, p1, *p3, k2tog, p1, k1, p1, yo, k1, yo, p1, k1, p1, ssk, p4, rep from * to marker, remove marker, p3, k2tog, p1, k1, p1, yo, k1, yo, p1, k1, p1, ssk, p2, kyok, k2.
Row 26: K2, yo, k1, pm, *k4, p1, k1, p1, k1, p3, k1, p1, k1, p1, k3, rep from * to last 4 sts, k1, pm, k1, yo, k2.
Row 27: K2, kyok, purl to marker, slm, p1, *p2, k2tog, p1, k1, p1, k1, yo, k1, yo, k1, p1, k1, p1, ssk, p3, rep from * to marker, slm, purl to last 3 sts, kyok, k2.

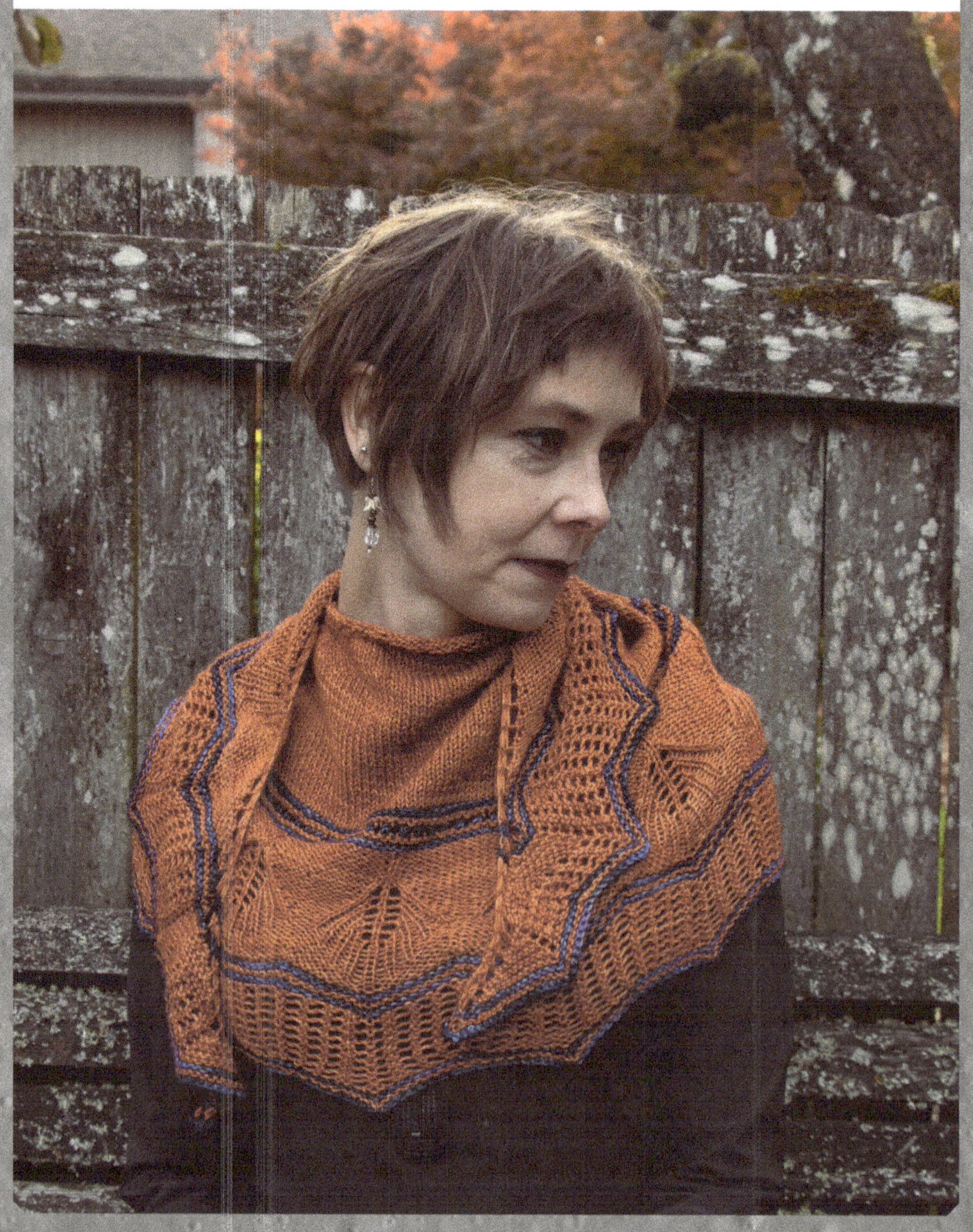

Row 28: K2, yo, knit to marker, slm, *k3, p1, k1, p1, k1, p5, k1, p1, k1, p1, k2, rep from * to 1 st before marker, k1, slm, knit to last 2 sts, yo, k2.
Row 29: K2, kyok, purl to marker, slm, p1, *p1, k2tog, p1, k1, p1, k1, p1, yo, k1, yo, p1, k1, p1, k1, p1, ssk, p2, rep from * to marker, slm, purl to last 3 sts, kyok, k2.
Row 30: K2, yo, knit to marker, slm, *k2, p1, k1, p1, k1, p1, k1, p3, k1, p1, k1, p1, k1, p1, k1, rep from * to 1 st before marker, k1, slm, knit to last 2 sts, yo, k2.
Row 31: K2, kyok, purl to marker, slm, p1, *k2tog, [p1, k1] three times, yo, k1, yo, [k1, p1] three times, ssk, p1, rep from * to marker, slm, purl to last 3 sts, kyok, k2.
Row 32: K2, yo, knit to marker, slm, *k1, p1, rep from * to 1 st before marker, k1, slm, knit to last 2 sts, yo, k2.
Row 33: K2, kyok, purl to marker, slm, p1, *p2, k1, [p1, k1] six times, p3, rep from * to marker, slm, purl to last 3 sts, kyok, k2.
Row 34: K2, yo, knit to marker, slm, *k3, p1, [k1, p1] six times, k2, rep from * to 1 st before marker, k1, slm, knit to last 2 sts, yo, k2.
Row 35: K2, kyok, purl to marker, slm, p1, *p4, k1, [p1, k1] four times, p5, rep from * to marker, slm, purl to last 3 sts, kyok, k2.
Row 36: K2, yo, knit to marker, slm, *k5, p1, [k1, p1] four times, k4, rep from * to 1 st before marker, k1, slm, knit to last 2 sts, yo, k2.
Row 37: K2, kyok, purl to marker, slm, p1, *p6, k1, [p1, k1] twice, p7, rep from * to marker, slm, purl to last 3 sts, kyok, k2.
Row 38: K2, yo, knit to marker, slm, *k7, p1, [k1, p1] twice, k6, rep from * to 1 st before marker, k1, slm, knit to last 2 sts, yo, k2.
Row 39: K2, kyok, purl to marker, remove marker, p1, *p8, k1, p9, rep from * to marker, remove marker, purl to last 3 sts, kyok, k2.
Row 40: K2, yo, knit to last 2 sts, yo, k2.

Chevron Stripes
Switch to color B leaving color A attached.
Row 41: K2, kyok, k14, *m1, k7, cdd, k7, m1, k1, rep from * to last 16 sts, k13, kyok, k2.
Row 42: K2, yo, knit to last 2 sts, yo, k2.
Switch to color A leaving color B attached.
Row 43: K2, kyok, k17, *m1, k7, cdd, k7, m1, k1, rep from * to last 19 sts, k16, kyok, k2.
Row 44: K2, yo, knit to last 2 sts, yo, k2.
Switch to color B leaving color A attached.

Row 45: K2, kyok, k2, *m1, k7, cdd, k7, m1, k1, rep from * to last 4 sts, k1, kyok, k2.
Row 46: K2, yo, k4, pm, knit to last 7 sts, pm, k5, yo, k2.

Chevron Lace
Switch to color A. Either carry the color B along the edge, wrapping the yarns every other row, or cut the color B and reattach it later.
Row 47: K2, kyok, knit to marker, slm, *m1, k7, cdd, k7, m1, k1, rep from * to marker, slm, knit to last 3 sts, kyok, k2.

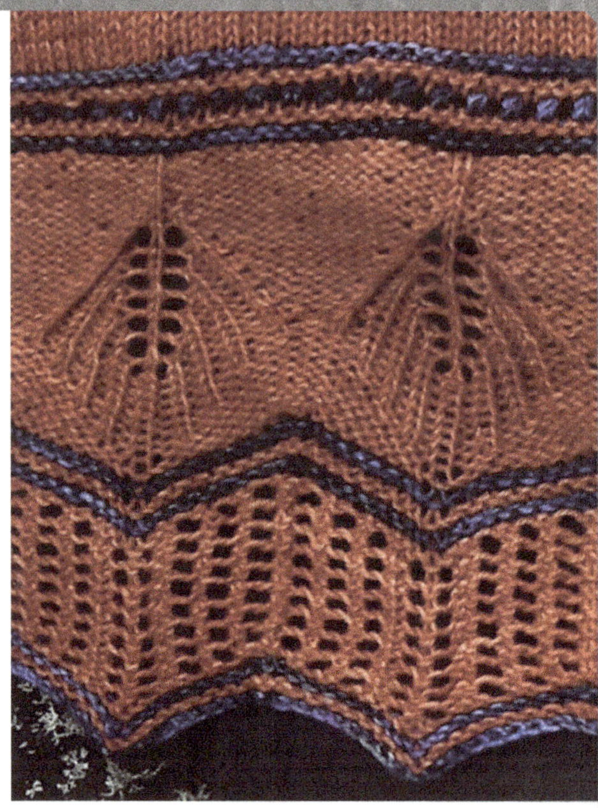

Row 48: K2, yo, knit to last 2 sts, yo, k2.
Row 49: K2, kyok, knit to marker, slm, *yo, k1, [ssk, yo] three times, cdd, [yo, k2tog] three times, k1, yo, k1, rep from * to marker, slm, knit to last 3 sts, kyok, k2.
Row 50: K2, yo, knit to last 2 sts, yo, k2.
Rep rows 49 and 50 three more times (four reps total) removing the markers in the last row.
Row 51: K2, kyok, k2, pm, *yo, k1, [ssk, yo] three times, cdd, [yo, k2tog] three times, k1, yo, k1, rep from * to last 4 sts, pm, k1, kyok, k2.
Row 52: K2, yo, knit to last 2 sts, yo, k2.
Rep rows 49 and 50 three more times removing the markers in the last row.

Rep rows 41 - 45 once.
BO all sts using the stretchy bind off on page 7.
Block gently, creating the crescent shape.

Faces of the Moon

The location and appearance of the moon in the sky is the result of an intricate dance among the moon, the earth, and the sun. The phases of the moon do not reflect actual changes in the moon, but rather are the result of changes in the angles between the earth, the moon, and the sun. One half of the moon is always illuminated by sunlight. Depending on the angle at which we view the moon, we see different parts of the illuminated surface, from a full moon to no moon at all.

Our ancestors learned to predict these changes, taking advantage of the moonlit nights of the full moon for some activities and waiting for the dark nights of the new moon for others. The Harvest moon is the full moon closest to the autumnal equinox. At this time of the year, moonrise is very soon after sunset, and the full moon provides extra light for farmers to work by while harvesting their crops.

The changing faces of the moon are woven throughout our mythology. The moon cycle is often tied to waxing and waning fertility, fortune, and sanity. One superstition says that when you see the first thin crescent after the new moon, you should take all your spare coins out of one pocket and switch them to another, thus ensuring good luck for the rest of the month. Others suggest that the full moon brings out werewolves and lunacy.

"O, swear not by the moon, th' inconstant
      moon,
That monthly changes in her circle orb,
Lest that thy love prove likewise variable."
      -William Shakespeare, *Romeo and Juliet*

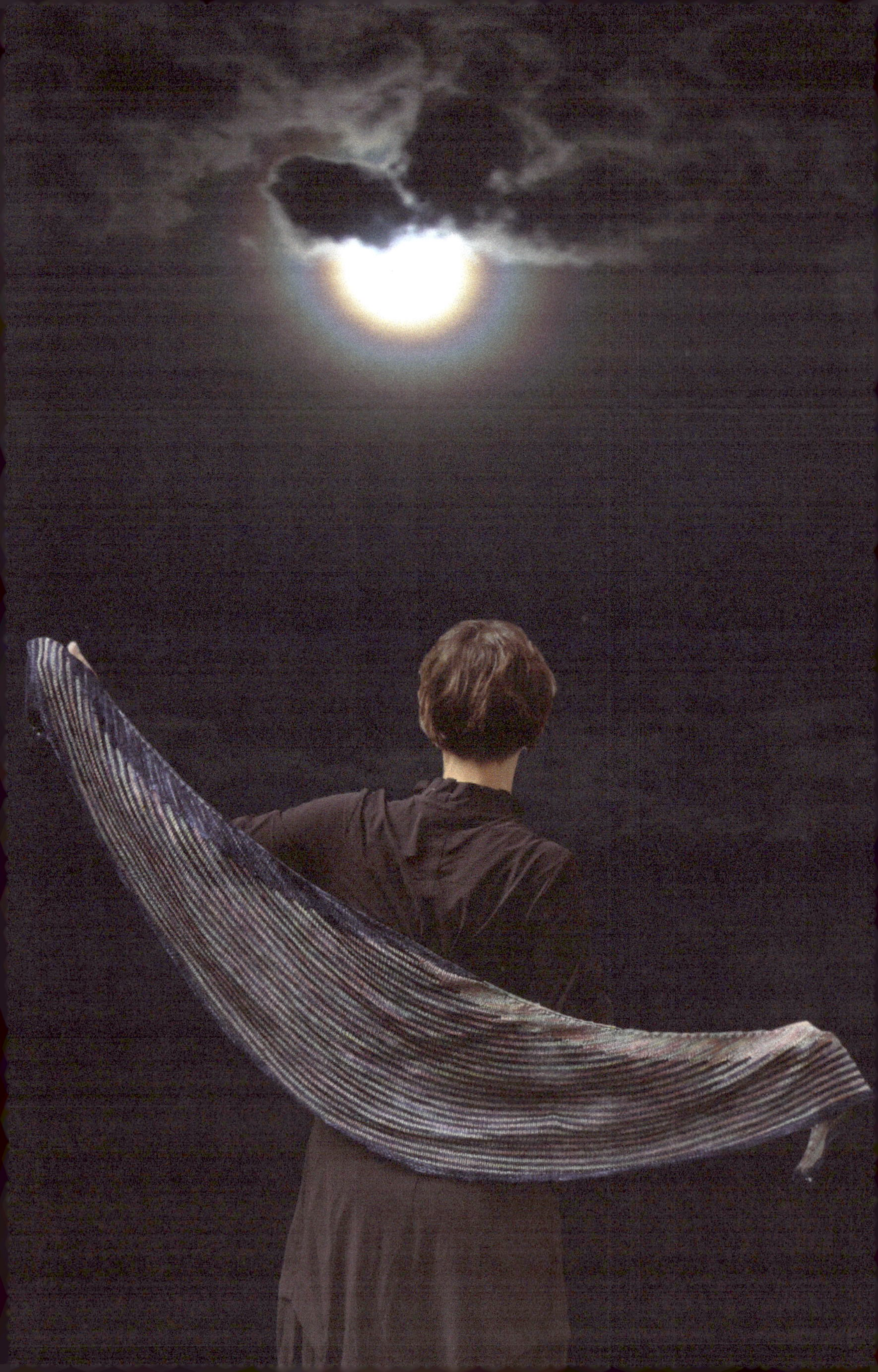

Moonbow

Alternating stripes of color interleave from opposite edges. Worked as short rows, each stripe falls a few stitches short of the opposite side, leaving bands of solid color at each edge.

Finished Measurements
Wingspan: 68 inches / 173 cm
Depth: 14 inches / 35.5 cm
Size is easily adjustable by using more or less yarn.

Materials
Yarn: Two colors of fingering weight yarn.
Shown in Dream in Color Smooshy; 85% superwash fine merino wool, 15% nylon; 420 yards/4 ounces
Color A: Indigo, 285 yards
Color B: Milky Spite, 220 yards

Needles: 40 inch US #5 / 3.75 mm circular needle, or size needed to obtain gauge

Tapestry needle

Gauge
18 sts = 4 inches / 10 cm in stockinette stitch

Special Stitches
Kyok (knit, yarn over, knit): Knit, then yo, then knit again into the same stitch. Three sts made from 1 st.

Ssp (slip slip purl) : Slip 1 st knitwise, slip a second st knitwise, return the 2 sts to the LH needle without further changing their orientation, purl the 2 sts together through the back loops.

Pattern

Set up
With color A CO 20 sts.
Row 1 (WS): K2, yo, knit to last 2 sts, yo, k2.
Row 2 (RS): K2, kyok, knit to last 3 sts, kyok, k2.
Rep rows 1 and 2 once more.
Row 3: K2, yo, purl to last 2 sts, yo, k2.
Row 4: K2, kyok, knit to last 3 sts, kyok, k2. - 38 sts.
Row 5: K2, purl to the last 2 sts, yo, k2. (Note that you DO NOT make a yo at the beginning of this row.)

Leave yarn attached and push the sts to the opposite end of the circular needle so you are ready to work another WS row.
Switch to color B.
Row 6 (WS): K2, yo, p18, turn.
Row 7 (RS): Yo, knit to last 3 sts, kyok, k2.

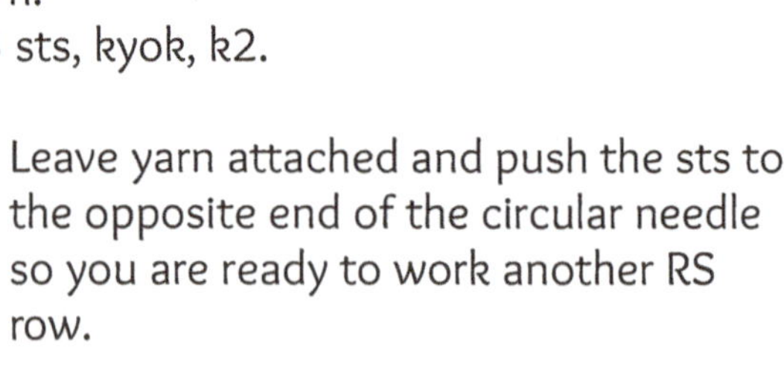

Leave yarn attached and push the sts to the opposite end of the circular needle so you are ready to work another RS row.

Body
Color A
Row 1 (RS): K2, kyok, k15, ssk, turn.
Row 2 (WS): Yo, purl to last 2 sts, yo, k2.
Row 3: K2, kyok, k19, k2tog, knit to last 19 sts, turn.

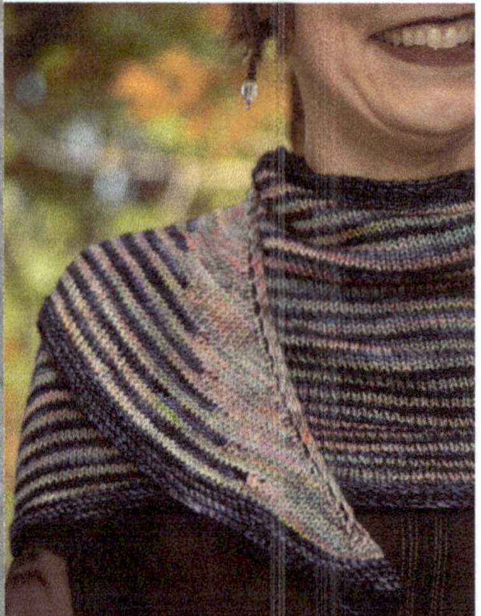

Row 4: Yo, purl to last 2 sts, yo, k2.
Leave yarn attached and push the sts to the opposite end of the circular needle so you are ready to work another WS row.

Color B
Row 1 (WS): K2, yo, p16, p2tog, turn.
Row 2 (RS): Yo, knit to last 3 sts, kyok, k2.
Row 3: K2, yo, p20, ssp, purl to last 19 sts, turn.
Row 4: Yo, knit to last 3 sts, kyok, k2.
Leave yarn attached
and push the sts to the
opposite end of the circular
needle so you are ready to
work another RS row.

Continue in pattern
alternating yarns until the
piece is approximately
13.5 inches tall (or desired
height) measured at the
center back. Be sure to stop
after a color B section. Cut
color B.

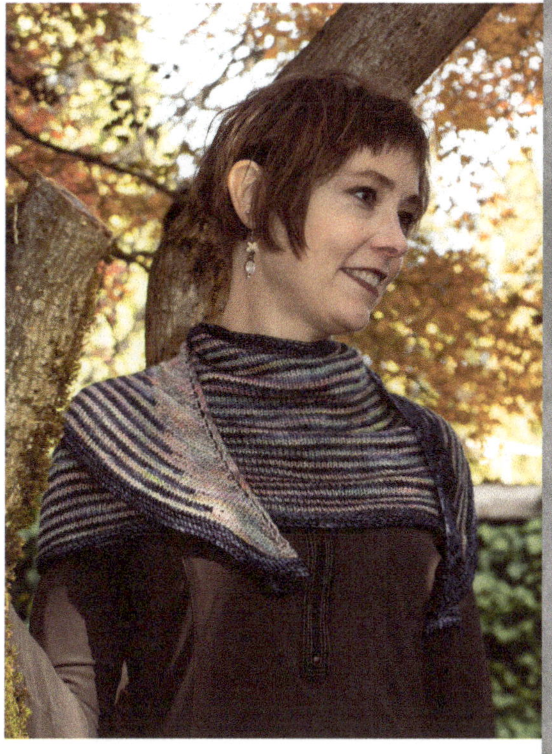

Edge
Color A
Row 1 (RS): K2, kyok, k15,
ssk, turn.
Row 2 (WS): Yo, purl to last
2 sts, yo, k2.
Row 3: K2, kyok, k19,
k2tog, knit to last 2 sts, yo, k2.
Row 4: K2, kyok, knit to last 2 sts, yo, k2.
Rep row 4 five more times (six reps total.)
BO all sts using the stretchy bind off on page 7.
Block gently, creating the crescent shape.

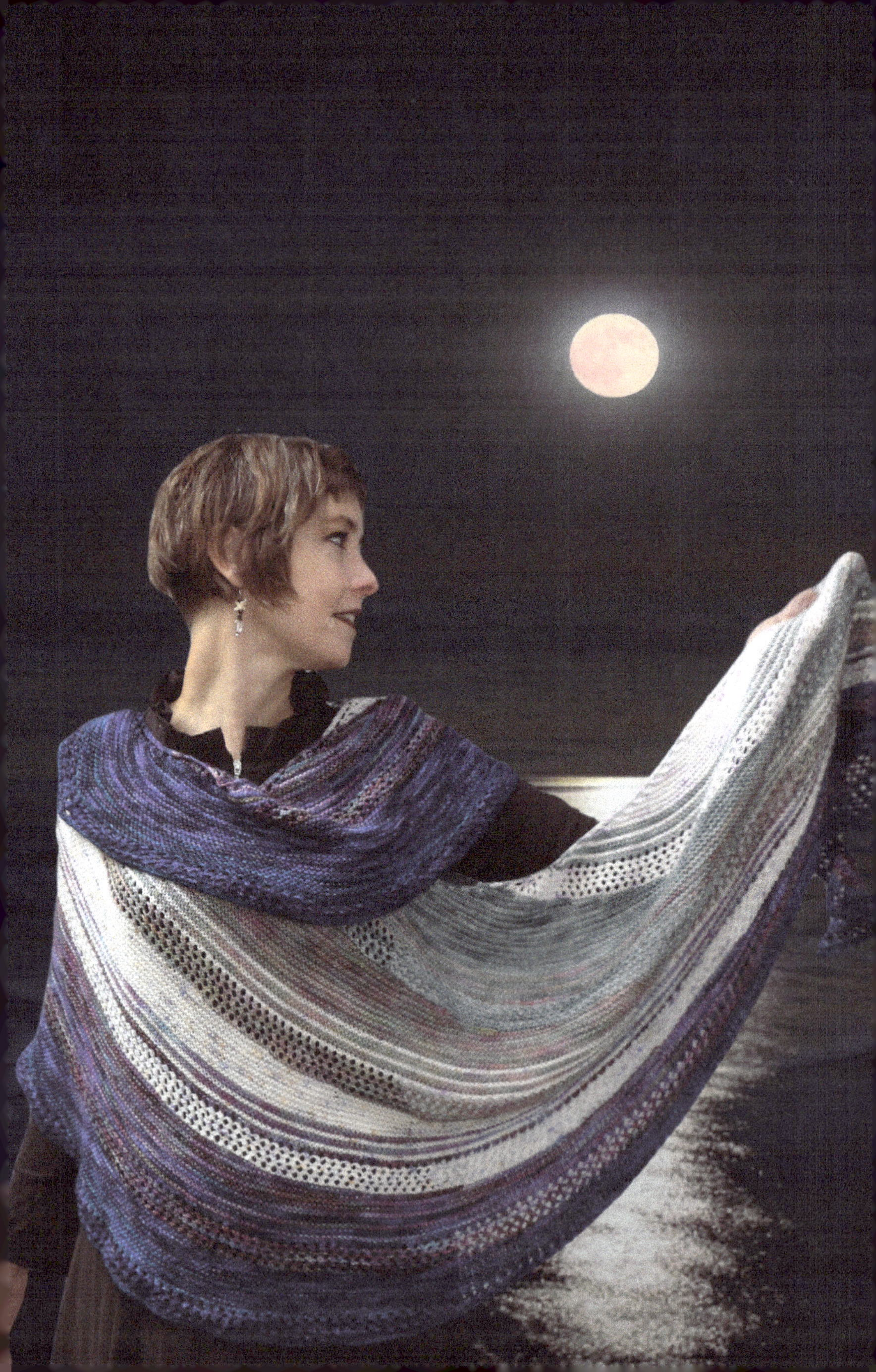

Moontide

In this color shifting shawl, short row wedges alternate with pretty
lace bands. Each color fades into the next with a series of stripes.
If you have chosen compatible colors, you can knit this shawl using
leftovers from the other patterns in the book.

FINISHED MEASUREMENTS
Wingspan: 90 inches / 228.5 cm
Depth: 20 inches / 51 cm

MATERIALS
Yarn: Seven colors of fingering weight yarn.
Shown in Dream in Color Smooshy; 85% superwash fine merino
wool, 15% nylon; 420 yards/4 ounces
Color 1: Still I Rise, 50 yards (Color B from Moonrise)
Color 2: Cedar Creek, 100 yards (Color A from Earthrise)
Color 3: Milky Spite, 155 yards (Color B from Moonbow)
Color 4: Whisper, 200 yards (Color C from Earthrise)
Color 5: My Fair Lady, 260 yards (From Moonbeams)
Color 6: Elysian, 330 yards (Color B from Harvest Moon)
Color 7: Blue Fish, 110 yards (Color B from Earthrise)

Needles: 40 inch US #4 / 3.5 mm circular needle, or size needed to
obtain gauge

Stitch markers
Tapestry needle

GAUGE
22 sts = 4 inches / 10 cm in garter stitch

SPECIAL STITCHES
Kyok (knit, yarn over, knit): Knit, then yo, then knit again into the
same stitch. Three sts made from 1 st.

The Pattern

First Wedge

With color 1, CO 6 sts.

Row 1 (RS): K2, yo, knit to last 2 sts, yo, k2.

Row 2 (WS): K2, kyok, knit to last 3 sts, kyok, k2.

Rep rows 1 and 2 until there are 78 sts.

Switch to color 2 and rep rows 1 and 2 once.

Switch to color 1 and rep rows 1 and 2 once.

Cont in pattern until there are 5 stripes (ending with a color 2 stripe.)
- 108 sts

Switch to color 1 and work one rep of lace section.

Lace Section

NOTE: At the start of each RS row, be sure to wrap the two yarns around each other so that the yarn that you are not knitting with will be caught up along the side of the work.

Row 1: K2, yo, k1, *yo, ssk, rep from * to last 3 sts, k1, yo, k2.

Row 2: K2, kyok, knit to last 3 sts, kyok, k2.

Rep rows 1 and 2 once more.

Row 3: K2, yo, k2, *yo, ssk, rep from * to last 4 sts, k2, yo, k2.

Row 4: K2, kyok, knit to last 3 sts, kyok, k2.

Rep rows 3 and 4 once more.

Rep rows 1 and 2 once more.

10 rows total worked.

Proceed to the next wedge.

At the end of each lace section you will have the following number of stitches.

Color 1 rep: 138 sts

Color 2 rep: 228 sts

Color 3 rep: 318 sts

Color 4 rep: 408 sts

Color 5 rep: 498 sts

Color 6 rep: 588 sts

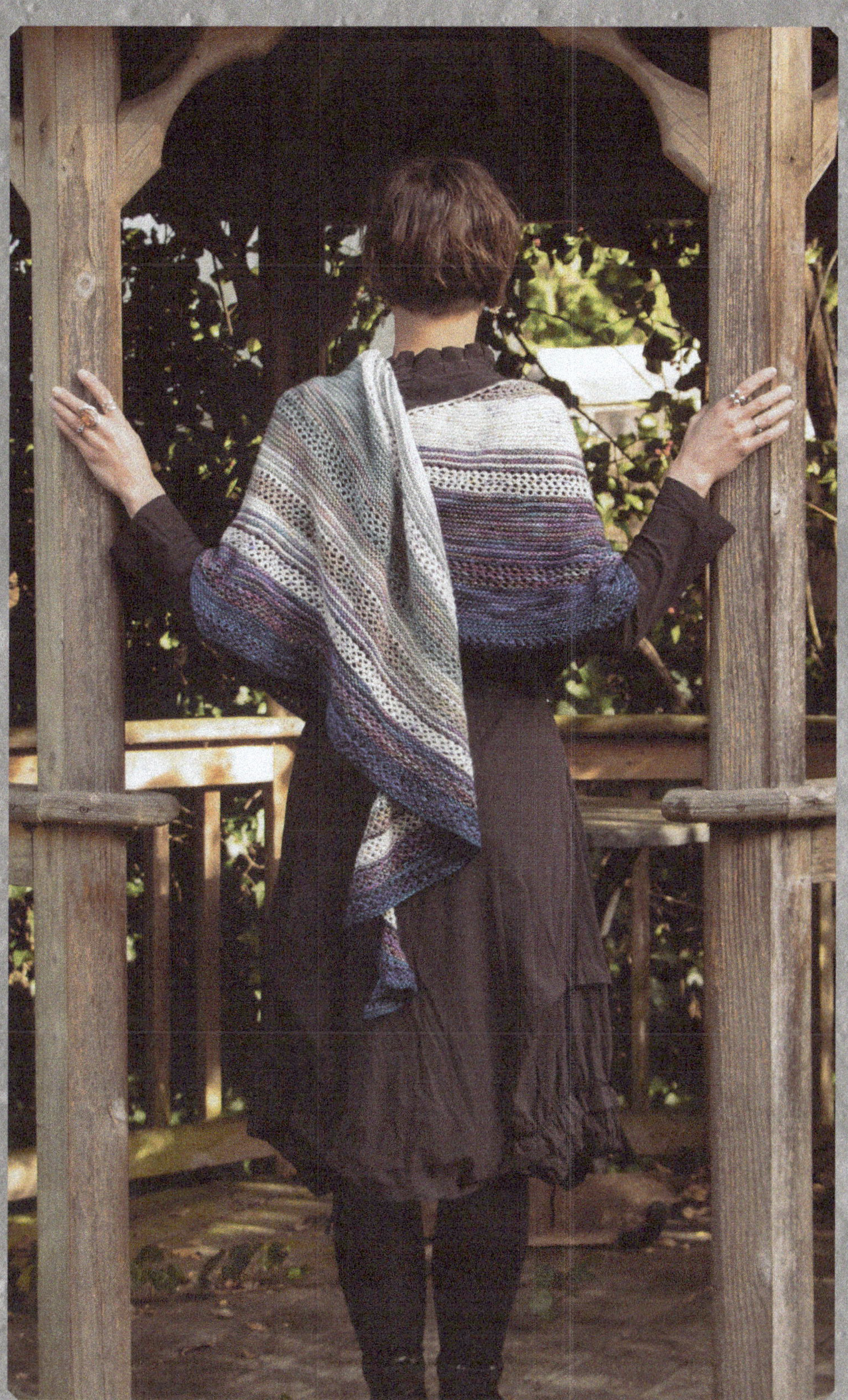

Moontide 47

Second Wedge
Cut color 1. Switch to color 2 and work short rows as follows.
Row 1: K2, yo, k5, turn.
Row 2: Yo, knit to last 3 sts, kyok, k2.
Row 3: K2, yo, knit to yo from the start of the previous row, k2tog, k6, turn.
Row 4: Yo, knit to last 3 sts, kyok, k2.
Rep rows 3 and 4 twelve more times (14 short rows worked.)
Switch to color 3 and rep rows 3 and 4 once.
Switch to color 2 and rep rows 3 and 4 once.
Switch to color 3 and rep rows 3 and 4 once.
Switch to color 2 and rep rows 3 and 4 once.
Switch to color 3.
Row 5: K2, yo, knit to yo from the start of the previous row, k2tog, knit to last 2 sts, yo, k2.
Row 6: K2, kyok, knit to last 3 sts, kyok, k2. - 198 sts
Switch to color 2 and work one rep of lace section.

Third Wedge
Cut color 2. Switch to color 3 and work short rows as follows.
Row 1: K2, yo, k10, turn.
Row 2: Yo, knit to last 3 sts, kyok, k2.
Row 3: K2, yo, knit to yo from the start of the previous row, k2tog, k11, turn.
Row 4: Yo, knit to last 3 sts, kyok, k2.
Rep rows 3 and 4 twelve more times (14 short rows worked.)
Switch to color 4 and rep rows 3 and 4 once.
Switch to color 3 and rep rows 3 and 4 once.
Switch to color 4 and rep rows 3 and 4 once.
Switch to color 3 and rep rows 3 and 4 once.
Switch to color 4.
Row 5: K2, yo, knit to yo from the start of the previous row, k2tog, knit to last 2 sts, yo, k2.
Row 6: K2, kyok, knit to last 3 sts, kyok, k2. - 288 sts
Switch to color 3 and work one rep of lace section.

Fourth Wedge
Cut color 3. Switch to color 4 and work short rows as follows.
Row 1: K2, yo, k14, turn.
Row 2: Yo, knit to last 3 sts, kyok, k2.
Row 3: K2, yo, knit to yo from the start of the previous row, k2tog, k15, turn.
Row 4: Yo, knit to last 3 sts, kyok, k2.
Rep rows 3 and 4 twelve more times (14 short rows worked.)
Switch to color 5 and rep rows 3 and 4 once.
Switch to color 4 and rep rows 3 and 4 once.
Switch to color 5 and rep rows 3 and 4 once.
Switch to color 4 and rep rows 3 and 4 once.
Switch to color 5.
Row 5: K2, yo, knit to yo from the start of the previous row, k2tog, knit to last 2 sts, yo, k2.
Row 6: K2, kyok, knit to last 3 sts, kyok, k2. - 378 sts
Switch to color 4 and work one rep of lace section.

Fifth Wedge
Cut color 4. Switch to color 5 and work short rows as follows.
Row 1: K2, yo, k19, turn.
Row 2: Yo, knit to last 3 sts, kyok, k2.
Row 3: K2, yo, knit to yo from the start of the previous row, k2tog, k20, turn.
Row 4: Yo, knit to last 3 sts, kyok, k2.
Rep rows 3 and 4 twelve more times (14 short rows worked.)
Switch to color 6 and rep rows 3 and 4 once.
Switch to color 5 and rep rows 3 and 4 once.
Switch to color 6 and rep rows 3 and 4 once.
Switch to color 5 and rep rows 3 and 4 once.
Switch to color 6.
Row 5: K2, yo, knit to yo from the start of the previous row, k2tog, knit to last 2 sts, yo, k2.
Row 6: K2, kyok, knit to last 3 sts, kyok, k2. - 468 sts
Switch to color 5 and work one rep of lace section.

Sixth Wedge
Cut color 5. Switch to color 6 and work short rows as follows.
Row 1: K2, yo, k24, turn.
Row 2: Yo, knit to last 3 sts, kyok, k2.
Row 3: K2, yo, knit to yo from the start of the previous row, k2tog, k25, turn.
Row 4: Yo, knit to last 3 sts, kyok, k2.
Rep rows 3 and 4 twelve more times (14 short rows worked.)
Switch to color 7 and rep rows 3 and 4 once.
Switch to color 6 and rep rows 3 and 4 once.
Switch to color 7 and rep rows 3 and 4 once.
Switch to color 6 and rep rows 3 and 4 once.
Switch to color 7.
Row 5: K2, yo, knit to yo from the start of the previous row, k2tog, knit to last 2 sts, yo, k2.
Row 6: K2, kyok, knit to last 3 sts, kyok, k2. - 558 sts
Switch to color 6 and work one rep of lace section.

Finish
Cut color 6 and switch to color 7.
Row 1: K2, yo, knit to last 2 sts, yo, k2.
Row 2: K2, kyok, knit to last 3 sts, kyok, k2.
BO all sts using the stretchy bind off on page 7.
Block gently, creating the crescent shape.

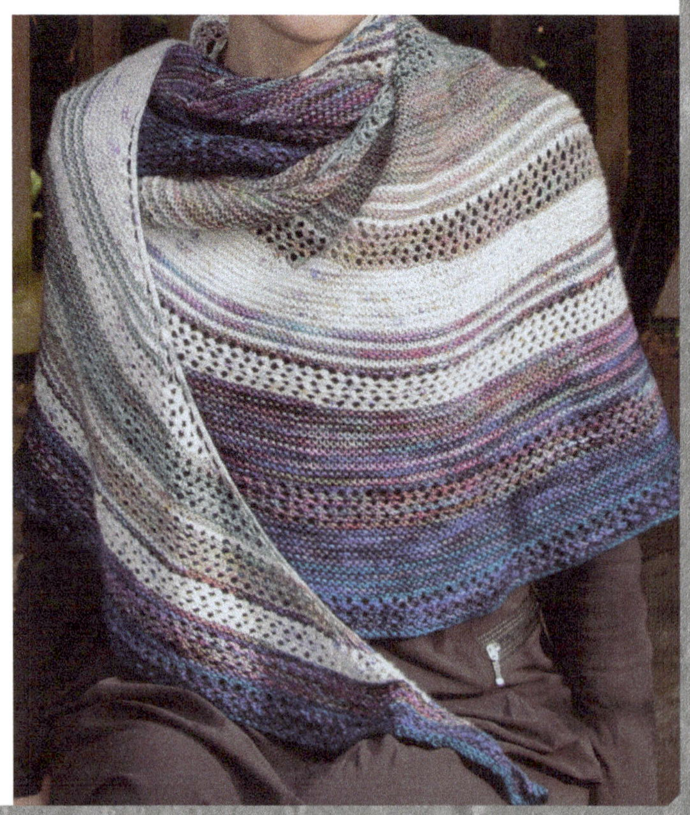

Cyclic Motion

Shining with unearthly light
Guiding beacon at nightfall
Cyclic motion wax and wane

Mystic spectral magic girds
Coven in ancestral hall
Shining with unearthly light

Speaking volumes without words
Intuition swell and fall
Cyclic motion wax and wane

Soaring higher than the birds
Orbiting above them all
Shining with unearthly light

Five nineteenths and seven thirds
Reasoned logic needn't call
Cyclic motion wax and wane

Friend of celestial cattle herds
Feline fiddler and flatware pal
Shining with unearthly light
Cyclic motion wax and wane

-Stephen B. Gerken

Thank You!

A big thank you to Bailey and his mom, Diana MacIntosh, for letting us use their backyard for the photo shoot.

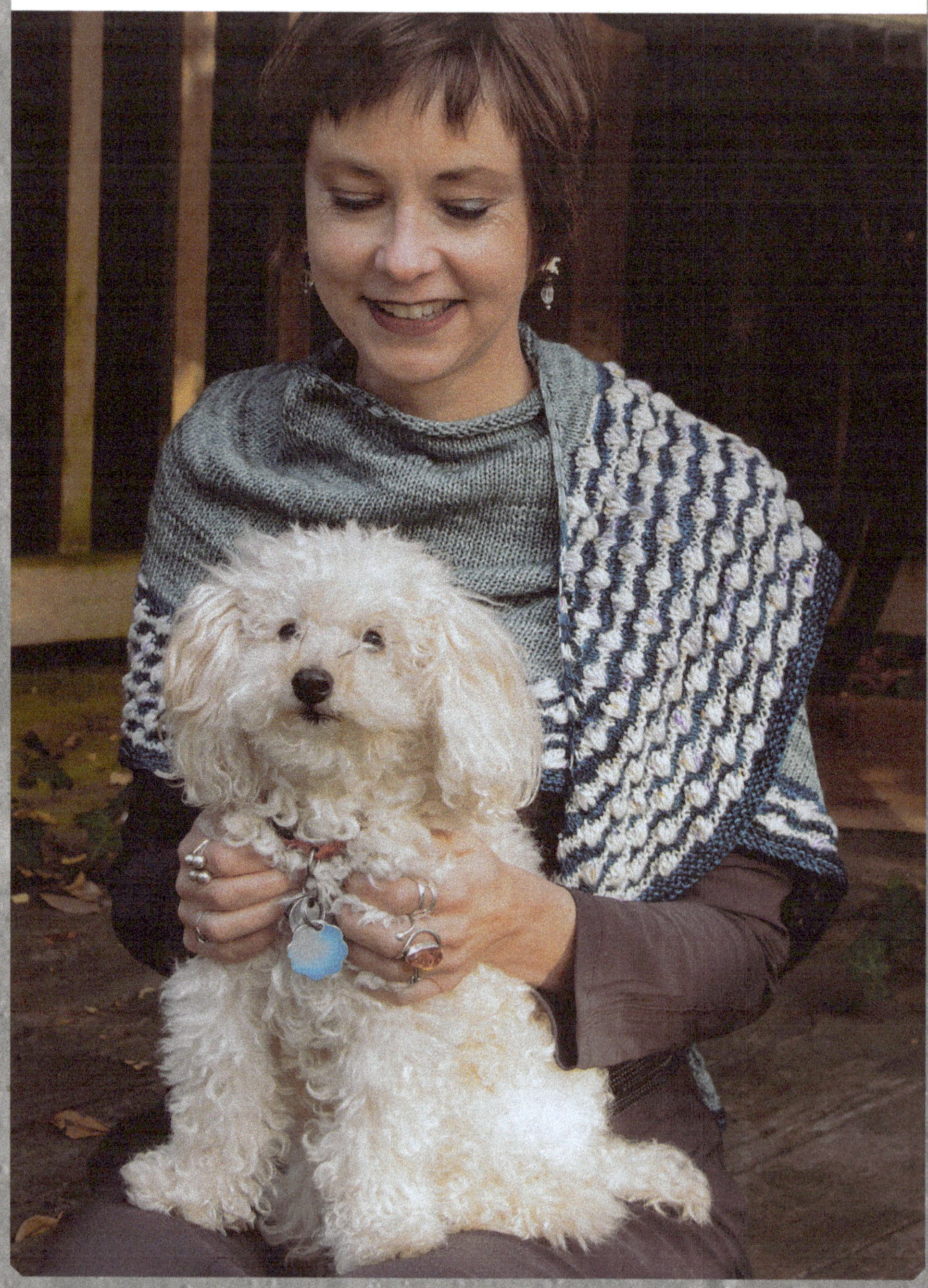

Acknowledgments

This book would not have happened without the help, support, and contributions of the following folks. Thank you!

To Stephen Gerken, my husband and my editor, thank you for agreeing to do this with me, again! And thank you for knowing which hat I needed you to wear on any given day.

To Marilyn Barnes, my photographer and my friend, thanks for being both.

To my lovely model, Robin Gill, thanks for being your wonderful self!

To my sample knitter, Kate Lindstrom, thank you for your beautiful and speedy work.

To my test knitters, Krashenne Asplodd, Su Fennern, Heather Hagen, Barbara Moncer, and Eva Schweber, thanks for your care and attention to detail.

To Dream in Color, who provided ALL the yarn, thank you for your generosity and support.

To all my Kickstarter donors, thank you for taking a risk on this project.

Photo Credits

Page background: Large Impact Crater, Lunar Surface
Author: Lunar Reconnaissance Orbiter Team
Copyright: Public Domain

Dedication page: Astronaut bootprint on the lunar surface.
Author: NASA
Copyright: Public Domain

Pages 10-11 background: Untitled
Author: StockSnap from Pixabay
Copyright: Pixabay License

Pages 16-17 background: Full Moon from Thailand
Author: PEAK99
Copyright: Creative Commons Attribution 3.0 Unported

Page 20 and pages 22-23 background: Earthrise
Author: William Anders
Copyright: Public Domain

Pages 26-27 background: Phases of the Moon
Author: Alex Andrews
Copyright: Pexels License

Pages 32-33 background: Moon rise over the Green River and sage
steppe at Seedskadee National Wildlife Refuge
Author: USFWS Mountain-Prairie
Copyright: Public Domain

Pages 40-41 background: Moonbow Over Black Rock City
Author: BLM Nevada
Copyright: Creative Commons Attribution 2.0 Generic

Pages 44-45 background: The moon in the waves
Author: Claudia Dea
Copyright: Creative Commons Attribution 2.0 Generic

All images have been resized and cropped.

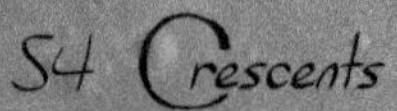
54 Crescents

About the Author

Theressa Silver is a freelance designer, teacher, and author of *Knitting Wild*. She has designed for magazines including *Jane Austen Knits* and *Enchanted Knits*. She is a contributor to the Knit Picks Independent Designers Program. She also has an array of self-published patterns available on Ravelry under the name ArgentGal Designs. Theressa is a biologist by training and the influence of math and science can be seen in many of her designs. When she is not knitting she likes to be outside kayaking or hiking. She has been known to stop on the trail, stare at something for a bit, and then exclaim, "I bet I could knit that!" She lives in Milwaukie, OR with her husband, two cats, and a dog, all of whom occasionally participate one way or another in the knitting process.

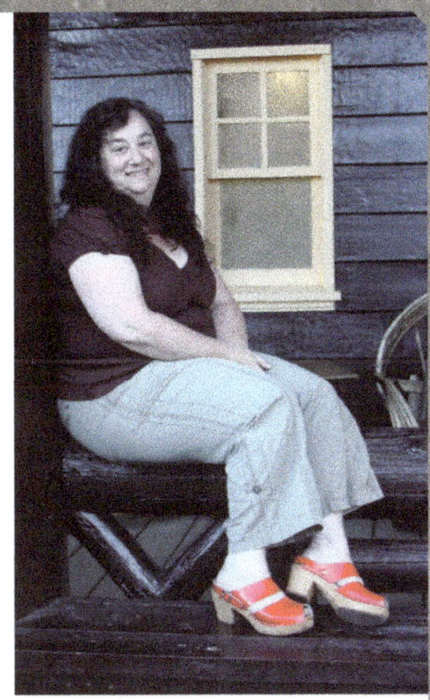

Theressa (aka Mom)
at Glacier Park Lodge
Photo: ©Samuel Silver

About the Photographer

Marilyn Barnes began taking photos when her grandchildren were born and quickly developed an interest in nature photography. A self professed "details person," she has a wonderful eye for texture and color and takes spectacular close-ups of plants and animals, many of which she sells as note cards. Over the years some of her favorite subjects, besides her grandchildren, have included roses, birds, butterflies, and dragonflies. A knitter of fifty years, when she isn't behind the lens of a camera, she's likely to have a pair of knitting needles in her hands. Marilyn lives in Milwaukie, OR and can be found riding her bike around town with her camera safely tucked in her saddle bag, or at the local coffee shop knitting with the girls.

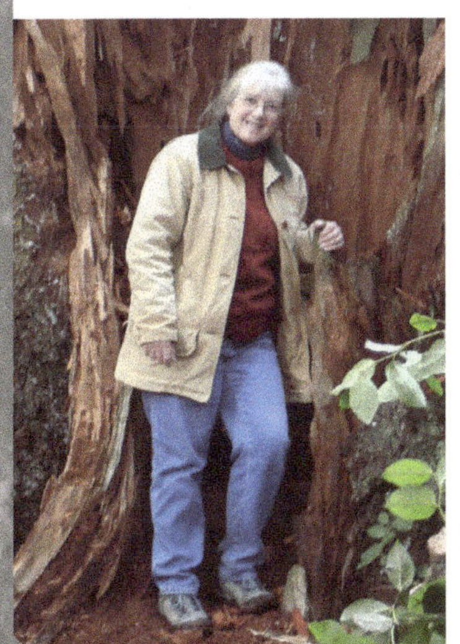

Marilyn at Cape Lookout State Park, OR
Photo: ©Dale Barnes